Gary Elson and O

Catfish

Everything About Natural History,
Purchase, Health Care, Breeding,
and Species Identification

Filled with Full-color Photographs
and Illustrations

BARRON'S

²CONTENTS

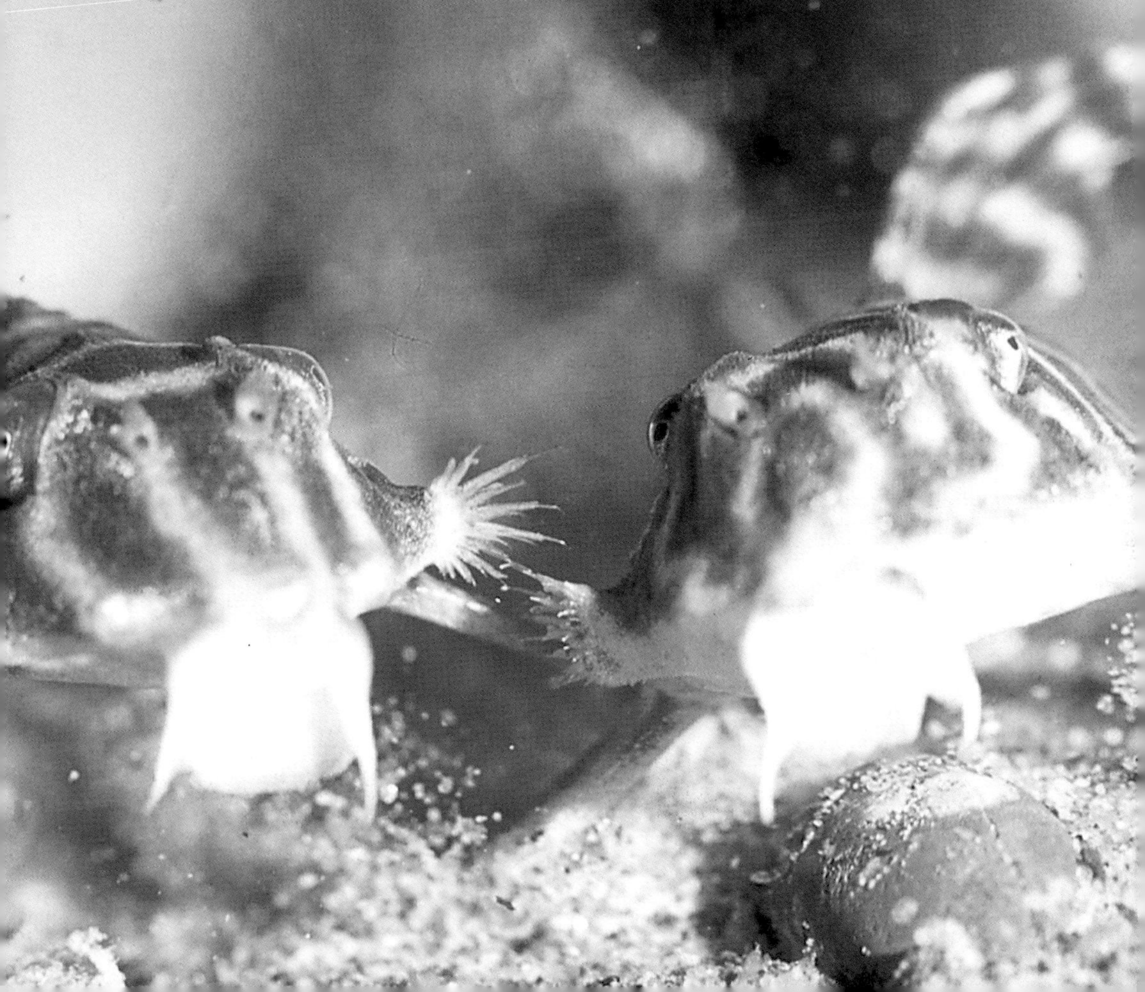

AN INTRODUCTION TO CATFISH

Catfish keeping usually starts as an afterthought. Quickly, though, it develops into a joyful hobby.

Becoming a Hobbyist

The hobbyist begins with a community tank, filled with brightly colored schooling fish. The traditional community setup calls for one or two catfish to occupy the bottom level of the tank and eat the leftovers. So a couple of these fish go in for a purely functional purpose. Then the fish-watching begins. Suddenly, the schooling fish look dull. The oddball cleaners on the bottom begin to assert themselves as fish like, and unlike, any others. As unscientific as it is, fish keepers begin to see that ill-defined attribute called "personality" in the new fishes. They begin to delight in keeping schools of perky, sociable Corydoras, or prehistoric looking bristlenoses.

It is not a development that was expected in the early days of the hobby. Older aquarium literature did not provide a lot of information about catfish. The writers never expected that

This is a typical **Farlowella** *habitat in Venezuela.*

catfish would someday be enormously popular, or that so many intriguing new species would be found. The keeping and observing of these fishes in the home aquarium has become such a popular hobby because each species presents its own challenges and each allows for the aquarist to make his or her own discoveries.

While faced with the complexity of the group, this manual will concentrate on catfish as aquarium inhabitants. It will deal with catfish of all types, provided they can be kept in the average small to mid-sized home aquarium. This will be based on an arbitrary maximum size limit of 8 inches (20 cm) in total length. Most of the fish in this manual will be much smaller than that. The species presented will be some of the popular smaller catfish in the huge family tree of the Siluriformes. Some groups have relatively few representatives among aquarium catfish:

Bagridae, including some of the Asian species in the genus *Mystus;*

Siluridae, or true catfish, which includes the glass catfish *(Kryptopterus)*;

Schilbidae, including the *Eutropiellus;*

Amphiliidae, including *Phractura;*

Helogenidae, including the woodcats *(Helogenes).*

Other genera have many species that fit well within the parameters chosen:

Mochokidae, including the *Synodontis;*

Doradidae, including the raphael catfish;

Auchenipteridae, including *Tatia;*

Aspredinidae, including the banjo catfishes *(Bunocephalus);*

Pimelodidae, including *Pimelodus;*

Callichthyidae, including the many *Corydoras, Aspidoras,* and *Brochis;*

Loricariidae, including the many "pleco" species in this book.

Diversity

Catfish diversity means the average aquarium store can have creatures from many habitats. Some are active by day and are front and center in any community tank. Others come out only at night or dusk, or they even hide in the sand or under decorations. If there is a niche that will allow a fish to prosper, chances are that somewhere along the long evolutionary path these animals have taken, at least one species will have developed the ability to exploit that environment. Cory cats can be among the gentlest inhabitants a community tank can have. In the wild, these gregarious schooling cats burrow through the top layer of sand and mulm looking for tiny foods. The same pet shop that sells 2-inch (5 cm) *Corydoras aeneus* may offer very young 2-inch (5 cm) red-tail cats. These are a gigantic predatory catfish from the Amazon

that, while cute when young, will rapidly devour all its tank mates before having a try at the family cat. While most commonly available aquarium trade live-bearers, characins (tetras), gouramis, or barbs are in the "what you see is what you get" category, quite a few catfish are like the equally popular cichlids in their ability to overwhelm the resources of the unwary aquarist. A good rule for the catfish keeper is that only what has been researched and read up on is what should be purchased. Hopefully, this manual will be a good step in that direction.

Understanding Catfish Names

For people starting out in the aquarium hobby, the use of Latin names for catfish may look very pretentious. Why call a spotted catfish *Corydoras paleatus* when spotted catfish will do? The problem is that in some regions, this one fish is called a salt and pepper cat, a paleatus cat, or just an armored cat. The number of species traveling under the "armored cat" name is astounding. When we consider that *Corydoras paleatus* is a bit of an anomaly as far as readily available tropical fish go, in that it needs cooler water than most related species, the need for precision for those who want to take good care of their fish becomes clearer. Many petshops sell "green Cory cats" that should be *Corydoras aeneus* but can be *Brochis splendens* or other fish that are hard to identify without information on where they originate. The Latin or scientific name is essential as an internationally understood and accessible code to allow the aquarist to seek precise information on a fish. Latin serves as a good neutral choice as it is no one's spoken language.

Following the system devised by Carolus Linnaeus in the late eighteenth century, a species will be grouped with all closely related animals in a genus (i.e., *Corydoras*). Each defined and distinct group of animals will have a species name (i.e., *aeneus*). The name of the individual who described the animal and the year of the description are added, as in *C. aeneus* (Gill 1858), for those who might want to look up the original study of the animal. This can be followed by either a subspecies name or an informal geographic location (i.e., *Corydoras aeneus* "orange stripe" or "Trinidad").

Oftentimes, a species will appear in the hobby before it has been scientifically studied. The usual presentation of such a fish is genus followed by a temporary species designation. This will give us, as an example, "*Corydoras* sp. Rio Santiago." We know where the fish is from and what genus it is in, but we are admitting our knowledge stops there. A similar approach is sometimes seen with the use of cf. or sp. aff. designations. A fish is found that looks like a known species, but for a variety of reasons, those who study the fish are uncertain about its exact identity. Such a species could be listed as *Corydoras* sp. aff. *aeneus* or *Corydoras* sp. cf. *aeneus*. What looks like pseudoscientific posing can carry important information for those breeding or maintaining species over the long term. It is certainly useful for avoiding possible crossbreeding of poorly defined or researched animals.

The "L" designations attached to many undescribed *Loricariids* are another example of undescribed or newly discovered species being given temporary names. While a scientifically described animal has a more or less permanent name (the first part, the genus, may change as research progresses), a system like the "L" names is temporary. Those who get involved in *Loricariid* keeping tend to end up doing a lot of reading, simply to catch up on how the portrait of the group is filling in as scientists work through the incredible diversity of these intriguing creatures. The "L" designations that are so important to the understanding of *Loricariids* now may just be a footnote in future catfish books. Already, once common names like "L-46" (now *Hypancistrus zebra*) for the zebra pleco have been replaced by formal species descriptions.

For fish-keeping purposes, genus and species are the essential information. The scientific name for a species is preceded by information on the broader relationships of the creature, an area where most hobbyists do not usually go, but which can be interesting.

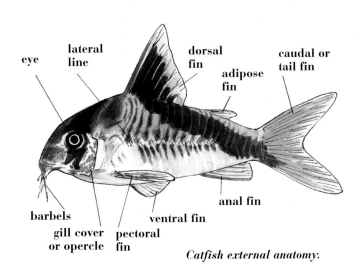

Catfish external anatomy.

CATFISH DISTRIBUTION

Catfish come from an incredible number of habitats. This section will take a quick look at some of the environments where popular species can be found.

Exotic Origins

The catfish kept in home aquariums come from some very exotic places. Indeed, they come from almost all habitats where fish can flourish, from seawater to the purest, softest rain forest waters. Although there are temperate species of great interest to the specialist, the species found in the hobby come from the tropics, largely from South America, Asia, and Africa. Partly this is a function of their role as tropical community tank dwellers and partly because there is no organized fish-collecting industry in cooler countries, even if interesting aquarium fish are there. The good news is that getting fish almost exclusively from tropical regions is not a terribly limiting factor. Cats occupy some weird and wonderful niches in the waters of the tropics. The diversity of their habitats matches the diversity of their shapes,

This **Plecostomus** *habitat on the Orinoco is located along the Colombia/Venezuela border.*

sizes, and behavior. While such habitats cannot be exactly reproduced in the aquarium, they provide excellent clues as to how these animals should be kept.

A Variety of Habitats

Amazonian woodcat habitats: The waters of the Amazonian rain forest move in a seasonal boom and bust pattern, filling the forests during the rainy season and retreating once the dry season arrives. As the floodplain retreats, it breaks into a series of streams. As the dry season advances, these streams are reduced to mere trickles, usually with shallow, sandy, leaf and tree branch-bottomed lakes at their mouths. The soft inner cores of the many fallen and submerged trees begin to break down, and increasingly hollowed logs with many entry points litter the lake bottoms. The sunken wood becomes a perfect habitat for all sorts of nocturnal fishes, including a wide variety of catfish.

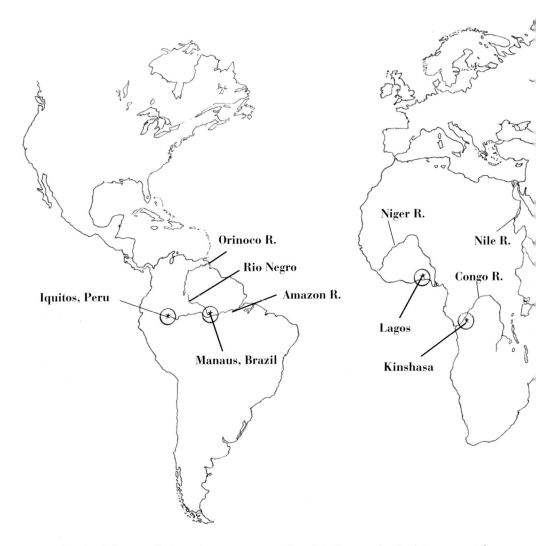

The lifestyle of the so-called woodcats revolves around decaying wood. The habitat of fallen trees provides them with cover, breeding spaces, and food. At night, many catfish species wander out to feed on tiny freshwater shrimp and the young of sleeping tetras and other fish. The popular Ancistrus are not fry predators, but many of their less well-known woodcat neighbors are.

When fish collectors enter the tea-colored waters, manageable logs are hauled out and broken up, causing hundreds of surprised cat-

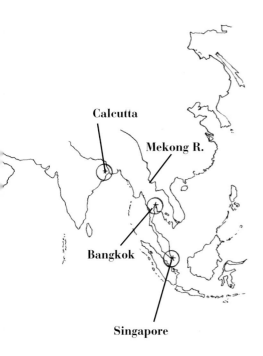

Calcutta

Mekong R.

Bangkok

Singapore

Catfish species sought after in the aquarium hobby are distributed throughout the tropical rivers of the world.

fish to come tumbling out. The dominant species in the logs of Brazil's Rio Negro are pimelodids, auchenipterids such as the naked catfish *(Tatia),* Pseudopimelodus (bumblebee cats), and some predatory Crenicichla pike cichlids. Ancistrus of all sizes are found and

collected in large numbers in this manner. The large males lodge themselves in their crevices using their ventral fins and can be hard to remove. As would be expected, these are territorial homebodies in the home aquarium too.

Obviously, trying to keep decaying wood in a home aquarium is not a good idea, but a few good pieces of drift or bogwood will go a long way toward making these animals seem happy. To keep groups of the fish, you will need a quite large home aquarium, with ample territories for all the males. Not all are safe community fishes, as will be seen in the species descriptions that follow.

A floating meadow: Amazonia has some features aquarists might not expect, including what are commonly called floating meadows. These reed beds (sometimes called portable islands) can even be found drifting down the main channels of major rivers. They are homes to a wide range of birds, insects, frogs, and fishes, including one of the stranger looking aquarium catfish. The various Farlowella species are among the great twig mimics of the fish world—beautifully camouflaged curiosities with a dedicated following in the hobby. They can be found among the twigs and broken branches of the floating meadow. With them (and a wide variety of tetras, cichlids, and other popular fishes) we find one of the great algae eaters. Lively little otocinclus cats can be caught by the thousands in these habitats as well as in inhospitable looking environments along the banks of all sizes of rivers.

Creating a floating meadow in a home aquarium may be impossible. However, enjoyment of all these fishes can be increased by keeping them in a heavily planted tank, ideally with lots of light. Floating meadow species will

Mystus vittatus *is a common Asian catfish.*

This Peruvian mountain stream is a habitat of **Chaetostoma** *catfish.*

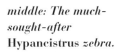

A Chaetostoma
specimen in the wild.

*middle: The much-
sought-after*
Hypancistrus *zebra.*

bottom: Peckoltia
*spec. L134, Tapajos
Tiger plecostomus.*

═══ TIP ═══

A Little Practical Catfish Anatomy

Catfish find their food in many ways. While many of our common aquarium fish rely largely on their eyes to spot food, catfish have an excellent sense of smell and can use their barbels as well as their lateral line organ on their flanks to find food. The barbels have nerve receptors and taste buds that allow catfish to locate food and prey at great distances—even in muddy water. Barbels are also important in the reproduction and courtship rituals of *Corydoras* catfish. The lateral line is a sensory organ unique to fish that allows them to sense minute wave vibrations. It is a largely exposed nerve that runs down the flank on both sides of the fish. This organ obliges thoughtful fish keepers to protect their fish from tapping on the aquarium glass and not to situate the tank in a high-traffic location likely to produce loud, stressful vibrations.

tend to stay in the vegetation, so plants should be chosen to grow at all levels of the tank. As would be expected for fish from the channels of rivers, they do best with a good current.

A Venezuelan stream habitat: Flowing water is a feature in another South American habitat type, in Venezuela, where *Farlowella* sp. are once again found, this time along with *Corydoras*. These fish live in small, clear water streams of the sort most aquarists would love to explore. Above water is jungle interspersed with rubber plantations. Amazon parrots fly over in pairs, hunting for food, while at dusk, howler monkeys earn their name. Where the sand becomes beach, thousands of butterflies soak up moisture. The bushes along the shore are full of insects, lizards, and fish-hunting snakes. The sandy bottom is often claimed by large *Geophagus* and *Satanoperca* cichlids. Above them is a constant interplay between predatory freshwater barracuda (*Acestrorhynchus*) and huge schools of open-water tetras.

Closer to shore, schools of chunky *Corydoras concolor* search the shallows for food. Tiny pink *Imparfinis* catfish live buried in the sand itself, along with knifefish of the genus *Rhamphichthys*. The tangled wood, roots, and twigs along the banks are full of beautifully camouflaged *Farlowella*. If these meandering streams have beds of bright green *Sagittaria* sp. growing in the slow bends and trailing flat along the surface, another surprise may await. Such brilliant green worlds are occupied by two species of equally green fishes, a small tetra of the genus *Ammocryptocharax* and the rare *Farlowella*-like green stick catfish, *Acestridium martini*.

In the flowing areas of the same streams, schools of silvery, needle-shaped *Iguanodectes geisleri* and *Hyphessobrycon* tetras dart through the bright light. The extreme murky shallows, with their accumulated leaf litter, are home to *Apistogramma* sp. "Breitbinden" and the dangerously opportunistic wolf tetra (*Hoplias*) species. We may not be able to bring this vibrant biotope to our homes; however, by building a community around *Corydoras* or *Farlowella* cats, we can enjoy many of its wonders.

Such a tank does not need to be deep. However, it should be heavily planted and feature as much bog or driftwood as possible. *Farlowella* (or for the very lucky aquarist, *Acestridium*) are the fish world's answer to stick insects. Their camouflage is astonishing, as is their breeding behavior. A tank with a sand bottom, a large school of cory cats, and a group of delicate *Farlowella* does not need tetras or cichlids to be eye-catching, but the addition of these fish would give the fish keeper a lot to enjoy watching.

Although authenticity is great, the aquarist should pass on adding the ultrapredatory wolf tetra.

An Amazonian stream habitat: In the early days of the aquarium hobby, it was assumed there were half a dozen species of *Corydoras* at most. Further exploration leaves it impossible to estimate how many different species there are. Pet stores may label species with the safe old names. However, a hobbyist with a discerning eye can regularly find undescribed species in the tanks of even ordinary shops. Imagine the situation in the wild, as these (generally) little fishes are very successful throughout the north of South America, all the way south to Uruguay. A traveling collector could find fish like the large and beautiful *Corydoras barbatus*, which cannot survive in heated aquariums, in cool coastal streams, while other species thrive in very warm shallow jungle streams. Some have surmised that for every stream in a given region, there can, in many cases, be a different *Corydoras* species. They are found in riffles, shallows, and feeder streams throughout the northern half of South America in all types of water.

Imagine the banks of a tributary of Brazil's whitewater Rio Branco at the low water point of the dry season. The many feeder streams are very hot, and the oxygen content is dropping. You could join the ever-present kingfishers in watching schools of thousands of corys traveling downstream. The small fish frequently come to the surface to breathe (they breathe with their intestines), constantly disturbing the surface. They can easily be scooped up with a hand net. In the clean but sediment-filled white water of the Rio Branco, only the corys' need to breathe surface air gives away their presence. Throughout all their varied habitats, it would rapidly become clear how wrong the clichéd view of corys as the garbagemen of the home aquarium is. These are active, sociable, schooling fish from clean water, which find their food in the sand along the bottom, much like many of the popular cichlids of the region.

A cory tank should recognize their need for cleanliness and for a sandy substrate that cannot damage their delicate barbels. The fact they can breathe surface air does not mean they can be overcrowded. At the same time, their gregarious natures must be respected. Based on what is both seen in nature and observed in the aquarium behavior of *Corydoras*, they should be kept in a school of at least six. The more *Corydoras* in a tank, the more amusing they will be. Kept alone, they are immobile, boring animals.

A river habitat: The shallow water along the banks of the Rio Tigre in Brazil has slow moving, very warm water. The absence of large fishes during the day is noticeable, but the shallows are teeming with fry of many species. When night comes, the scene changes radically. The shallows fill with fish, as *Pimelodus* cats with their long barbels move in to hunt. A flashlight will easily catch the green eyes and silvery bodies of *Pimelodus pictus*, even in the shallowest water. *Loricaria* move in from deeper water and sift the sand and detritus in search of small worms.

Peckoltia
*spec. LDA19,
Mega Clown
plecostomus.*

Loricaridae
*spec. L128,
the blue
plecostomus.*

Baryancistrus
*spec. L177,
gold nugget
plecostomus.*

Pimelodus pictus *is a scavenger par excellence.*

Hemidontichthys acipenserinus *sifts while hunting for small food animals.*

Synodontis eupterus *is an upside-down surface feeder.*

Fishermen throw the rotting heads of cattle into the water during the day to cash in on the well-known *Pimelodus* inability to resist a good scavenge. At night, nets are thrown over the bait, and hundreds of specimens can be caught at each site.

These popular but quick growing catfish need a spacious, well-filtered aquarium. *Pimelodus* sp. grow quite large and are often kept either on their own or in larger tanks with cichlids.

Bunocephalus habitats: The shallowest water in a rain forest stream collects a thick layer of fallen leaves. This dark and secret world is inhabited by the insects and small shrimp we would expect, but there are also catfish and dwarf cichlids thriving in this weird shadowy habitat. Many hobbyists have purchased a banjo catfish (*Bunocephalus* sp.) only to have it disappear for weeks on end before emerging healthy and happy one evening. Their origins provide a clue to their aquarium behavior. These fish avoid the bright world of the open water and will even go into the gravel to seek shelter. For these small fishes, bright light is glaring danger.

This specialized habitat and lifestyle has produced a wide number of surprising catfish. The genera *Bunocephalus*, *Amaralia*, *Dupuoyichthys*, *Microglanis*, and *Heptapterus* all share the leaf litter with juveniles of the ever-present fearsome predatory characin *Hoplias* and the popular dwarf cichlids of the genus *Apistogramma*. Anyone wishing to keep these fish has to be aware of their tastes for shadows and hiding places. If given lots of cover, they are much more likely to be seen than if they are forced to disappear behind a filter or burrow under the sand to feel safe. They will always need a tank with alternating light and shadows and with many hiding places. Because of their burrowing, a soft, fine, sandy substrate is good for them.

A deepwater habitat: The "zebra pleco" was quite a hit when it showed up in the hobby a few years ago. This tiny, black-and-white striped fish looks more like a candy than it does a catfish. In spite of its beauty and popularity, it has remained somewhat hard to find. A look at its habitat answers a lot of questions about why.

The Rio Xingu in Brazil is surprisingly large to those who have only glanced at it on maps. It is very impressive with its jungle-lined banks, at least in the stretches where logging, cattle rearing, or gold prospecting have yet to start their destruction. The presence of giant Amazon otters (not to mention many fish eagles) would lead us to expect the local fish to have good camouflage and highly developed survival strategies. Relatively recent exploration of these waters has yielded some delightful surprises.

In retrospect, the clear water and many islands might have offered clues to how many *Loricariid* species could exist there and nowhere else. However, scientists and aquarist collectors were still overwhelmed by the incredible influx of unknown catfish that came from this system. The same phenomenon happened when the neighboring Tocantins and Tapajos system were explored for fish. Collectors and hobbyists were obliged to create a number system (the "L" system, described in chapter 1), which has been picked up by the scientific community. This was extremely important as *Loricariids* come in all sizes, and telling them apart therefore becomes quite important for the aquarist. Not all these fish are the same small size as the zebra!

In the dry season, the water in the zebra pleco habitat gets to 100 to 130 feet (30 to 40 m) deep. Divers using long air-supply hoses connected to compressors laboriously search the bottom for *Loricariids*. Zebras live with the magnificent *Medusa pleco (Ancistrus ranunculus)* along the bottom between rocks. The divers pry the plecos out of their caves using short sticks and place them into linen bags. Visibility with a flashlight is 3 feet (1 m) or less.

In the shallower habitats closer to shore, the popular gold nugget plecos *(Baryancistrus)* species are collected by the hundreds.

In a similar-looking habitat along the whitewater Rio Orinoco along the Colombia-Venezuela border, *Lasiancistrus* are collected by snorkel divers who find the fish by reaching into murky crevices and locating the catfish by touch. It is easy to understand why these strange and beautiful *Loricariids* are more expensive than many other tropical fishes.

The deepwater catfish are best kept in extremely well-filtered tanks with extensive rock work along the bottom. They need a good, strong current.

An African river habitat: The upside-down catfish of the genus *Synodontis* are popular curiosities, very different in their habits from many of the South American cats. *Synodontis* cats come from the margins of flowing water in Central Africa, the Congo River basin, the Nile, Chad, Niger, Senegal, Gambia, and all the way down to the Zambezi River. The various species are widespread and share a preference for habitats with good plant growth and tangled roots, where they feed on crustaceans, plankton, insects, and plant matter. The rivers of this region tend to flood less than their Amazonian counterparts, but they still collect a lot of driftwood along their banks. In the aquarium, the Congo River's popular upside-down cats like to shelter and feed around driftwood arranged like roots descending from the surface down to the gravel. They are schooling fish that are not bottom oriented. Like many catfish, they prefer to feed after the Sun goes down.

An Asian open-water habitat: Asia gives us the wonderful, transparent glass catfish *Kryptopterus bicirrhis,* the nicest of the many fish traveling under the popular name "glass." These fishes break down a lot of the stereotypes about what a catfish is. They do not feed on the bottom and like to feed in the current below the surface. Their habitat is open, murky water in the Mekong Delta, the Malay Peninsula, Sumatra, and Borneo. In turbid water, their transparent bodies are beautifully camouflaged. These schooling catfish illustrate the adaptability of the grouping we call catfish. If nature offers a niche, chances are a catfish will find a way to prosper in it.

A fish that hides in the open water has its own needs, very different from South American woodcats or African upside-down cats. The beautiful shine that makes these semitransparent fish almost invisible in murky waters makes them attractive in the clean water of a well-maintained home aquarium. However, the clarity of the water means that in captivity, these are nervous animals.

As these examples illustrate, it is hard to approach catfish keeping with a set formula. The fish and their needs have to be studied before moving to the next stage—setting up a catfish aquarium.

THE CATFISH AQUARIUM

How a catfish aquarium is set up will depend on a wide range of factors. In most cases, captive catfish share their living quarters with lots of other popular types of fishes. In others, the hobbyist chooses to specialize, and keep only catfish, or only mixed groups of cats. Both approaches call for slightly different setups, but are still inspired by the basic principles of aquarium management.

The Basics

To begin, the fish keeper should choose the largest tank resources allow for. A big tank could be a 20 gallon (75 L), or a 50 gallon (190 L), depending on space, budget, and level of interest. However, it is always easier to have more room than is needed rather than not having enough. An overcrowded tank is a disaster waiting to happen (that will, unfortunately, happen quickly). While it may seem strange, people who would be horrified to keep dogs, birds, or other pets in filthy, overcrowded conditions will often suspend logic and jam fish into totally inappropriate containers. Overcrowding is a common trap for new fish keepers, as the variety of tropical fishes available can be extremely tempting. If one steps back and considers the welfare of the animals

ahead of the spectacle they may offer, it is easily avoided.

Larger tanks are not just prettier. They are easier to maintain, as the ratio of water to fish wastes is in the fish keeper's favor. They will give a new aquarist a bit more time to learn the basics of the water maintenance routine.

A good general rule is to calculate 1 inch (2.5 cm) of adult fish for each gallon (4 L) of well-filtered water. Most new fish keepers react by thinking this rule will leave them with empty tanks. However, if the goal in aquarium keeping is to have fish that show interesting behavior while staying healthy, it is a good rule of thumb. More fish can be put in, but this will oblige a lot more effort to be put into maintaining the aquarium.

For most catfish, it is the bottom of the tank that matters. Depth is not a key factor. The aquarist should look for a tank that allows for swimming room and for the maintenance of

Blackwater **Corydoras** *habitat in Peru.*

territories. Even a cory, with its habit of sitting on rocks or the gravel for long stretches, likes room to roam when the urge hits.

Filtration

The best low-cost, low-technology aquarium filters are alive. This may sound strange to a newcomer to the hobby, but biological filtration, which uses beneficial bacterial colonies to process wastes in water, is a well-established technology. To simplify the process greatly, a biological filter is a mechanical device designed to facilitate the feeding of certain types of bacteria. Their food comes from aquarium fish waste products. Nitrites and ammonia from

organic wastes and fish respiration can rapidly pollute the water in even a large aquarium. These chemicals can contribute to the development of diseases and parasitic illnesses in fish, as the animal's immune system is under constant stress. On its own, ammonia can kill or deform your fish. The microscopic life-forms that will colonize on a filter over the first three weeks of its functioning transform the toxins in fish wastes into less dangerous substances that can then be removed by the aquarist, with regular maintenance water changes. There are debates about which microorganism does what in the process. However, what matters to fish keepers is that the system, in its many forms, works efficiently.

The bacteria in a biological filter have to be cultivated, as the filter that comes from the store is lifeless. How this is done may be one of the most important lessons in the early phases of an aquarist's interest in the hobby. Many beginners kill their fish in the first month, with no idea of how they are accidentally doing this.

A biological filter must be cycled. This can be done naturally, by adding gravel or other bacterially colonized materials from an established tank at the start-up, then keeping the aquarium population low for the first month to give the new culture time to build up its mass. Bacteria starter cultures can be found in well-equipped pet shops. The efficiency of these products can vary, so hobbyists should still proceed cautiously when stocking a new tank.

For aquarists, filtration types can be classified as those easy to use and inexpensive to purchase, all the way up to advanced, more expensive systems often modeled after waste-

TIP

The Nature of Water

Water is different things in different places, depending on its source and what it comes into contact with. Most tropical catfish come from rain forests, and clean rain is free of minerals and chemicals. In rain forests, water mainly comes into contact with the decaying wood and leaves through which it flows. These release tannins and other organic acids into the water, producing a pH below 7.0, and a habitat known as blackwater. Similar habitats are found in freshwater forest streams and marshes around the world. The water is clean but stained.

The pH scale operates with 7.0 as neutral and with each point up (alkaline) or down (acidic) being a large jump in the chemistry of the water. While most Amazonian water is quite acidic, most urban tap water in the industrialized world is alkaline.

Water that flows through rocky habitats will generally pick up alkaline minerals from the substrate and will develop a higher pH (above the neutral point). This is carried to its extreme (for catfish) in the Great Lakes of East Africa, where trapped water with little outflow is very alkaline and rich in minerals. Fish adapt to their native water. This adaptation can take the form of physiological changes that affect immune systems and reproductive behavior. Many fish from blackwater have eggs that will not hatch in harder water. It is possible a fish from an extreme habitat may not adapt well to what is available in the home aquarium. Most catfish can tolerate a wide range of hardness and pH, but the "wrong water" will be a problem for some.

Modifying aquarium water is not an easy project. Doing it once is easy. However, to maintain stable water conditions through necessary maintenance water changes demands a lot of attention, care, and work. Water treatment systems are on the market to allow for a controlled source of water (reverse osmosis or resin-based systems can be excellent). However, most experienced hobbyists prefer to choose fish that will adapt to the conditions offered by the water they have readily available.

water treatment systems. There are also mechanical filtration systems, which simply remove visible wastes from the water but provide little biological activity. Hybrids between the two approaches are also available.

Simple Filter Designs

Probably the most common filter design across the aquarium world is the power filter. All are variations on a basic plan. A small electric motor spins an impeller, which draws water

Plecostomus collectors diving in the Rio Orinoco.

up a tube into a plastic box hanging on the back of the tank. In the box, the water passes through mechanical and biological filtration media, which can include sponges, special fibrous filtration media, activated charcoal, peat moss, or various chemically active resins. The water then overflows through a channel and drops back into the tank with enough force to agitate the surface and aid in the exchange of oxygen.

All the models on the market have their strong points but share the same potential weakness. Somewhere in this tiny system, there should be a biological filtration component to break down organic wastes. For this to work, the biological media must be of a reasonable size. Large power filters work infinitely better than small ones, especially when the large filter runs slowly enough to allow a large volume of water consistent contact with beneficial bacteria.

A wholesale change of the contents of the filter during cleaning will temporarily destroy the efficiency of a filter. The biological media should be reusable and easily rinsed in nonchlorinated water (sponges can be repeatedly squeezed out in a bucket containing water drawn from the aquarium). Some fish keepers use two filters, so they can be cleaned in alternance.

A variation on the outside box design is the slightly more expensive but very efficient and quiet canister filter. Here, the water is drawn into a sealed cannister, where it is subject to the same processes but with a much greater volume of filtration media. Canisters can be a little annoying to clean, although new designs on the market are more and more user-friendly. They do a great job as long as their convenience does not cause them to be ignored when the time comes to clean the tank.

Catfish have no problem with the outflow of water, although a strong current in a small tank can be fatal to other, usually highly inbred fish like veiltail guppies or long-finned Bettas. *Loricariids* need as much filtration as you can reasonably supply, while smaller cats like *Corydoras* seem to revel in a good run into a strong, oxygenated current. If you like larger herbivorous catfish, then you will need more powerful filters to deal with their wastes.

In all cases, you should follow the manufacturer's suggestions for matching your filter model with the size of your tank. You may save money in the short term with a smaller model, but you will likely lose fish. Remember that as a filter clogs (i.e., as it filters), the flow rates you see on the box will slow down quickly.

Undergravel filters are first-rate filtration systems if they are well-maintained. An undergravel filter is a perforated plastic plate put, as the name implies, under gravel (2 inches [5 cm] of medium coarse gravel is best). By using an air pump or ideally a power head (a small submersible water pump), water is drawn through the gravel, which quickly becomes a large biological filtration medium. With the constant pulling down of wastes, the gravel may become clogged, which is where maintenance comes in. Siphon-operated gravel vacuums can be bought in any good aquarium store, and they should be used with every water change. Undergravel filtration systems should be avoided for crowded tanks.

If you choose to keep banjo cats, or other burrowing catfish, forget about an undergravel. The fish can actually get under the filter plate and live healthy lives, permanently out of sight. One of the authors once put three banjo cats in a community, only to have them disappear, missing and presumed dead, for over six months. One day, for whatever reason, all three cats reappeared, twice as large as when they had disappeared, healthy and very welcome. As fish-watching experiences go, burrowing cats and filters they can live in offer a poor show.

Sponge filters are not new and they are not pretty, but they do their job very well. Mechanically, these filters consist of a tube with holes in it, with an attachment for air from a pump to create a suction. The action of the air forces water through a thick but porous sponge wrapped around the tube. The sponge is colonized by enormous numbers of beneficial bacteria. It is simplicity itself.

Aquarists rarely use these bulky and obvious filters in show tanks, but they are extremely common in breeding and fry-raising tanks. Along with water changes, they keep the tank healthy while not creating enough suction to trap newly hatched catfish or to disturb spawning.

Corner box filters: Sponge filters do not, however, provide efficient mechanical filtration. The best air pump-operated option for this is the corner box filter. These plastic boxes come in many sizes and are generally stuffed with activated charcoal and synthetic filter wool. With time, they provide some biological filtration. Generally, though, they are a slightly inefficient alternative to sponge filters in a set up where a slow water flow is necessary. Many aquarists use them in combination with sponge filters. Because of their low cost, they, like sponge filters, are very popular with aquarists who run multitank setups.

Complex Filters

To keep numbers of the larger *Loricariids* calls for larger, more efficient, and often more expensive filtration. Larger or multitank systems work well with wet-dry or trickle filters. These devices (often the size of an average aquarium) provide immense surfaces for beneficial bacteria while oxygenating the water. With proper plumbing (an art in itself), wet-dry filters are usually used on multiple tanks. Most of the time, they are designed for saltwater systems but are easily and effectively adapted to freshwater.

Heating

Not all aquarium catfish come from warm waters. However, the majority of cats like their water warmer than room temperature in the average temperate climate home. The market is full of heating options. Aquarium heating is not an area where one should buy the cheapest option, as in this important domain, consumers get exactly what they pay for. A cheap heater's thermostat can become stuck, eliminating its ability to shut off. As temperatures climb, the fish move from discomfort to oxygen starvation and, in the all-too-common worst case, to fish soup.

Submersible heaters are the best options, especially those with electronic controls. You should have 1 watt per 2 gallons (8 L) minimum, and if possible divide the load between two devices. Like lightbulbs, heaters do burn out with time. A sudden, calamitous drop in temperature can be avoided if you have a backup. Always unplug the devices before putting your hands into the aquarium.

For robust catfish species, buy a heater that is in a protective plastic cage and that attaches firmly to the glass. Some rowdy fish will decide to change the décor in their home, with potentially electrifying results.

With the heater comes the need for a good thermometer, which you should check a minimum of once daily. Outside of the tank, stick-on thermometers are very popular, but not all models are accurate or easy to read. Suction cup inside models have a tendency to float loose with time, especially if a robust species of catfish decides they would make a good plaything. Clip-on models can be adequate, but an electronic thermometer with a submerged sensor is the easiest to use and most efficient option.

Gravel

The type of gravel used in a catfish tank is more important than for most other fish. While many aquarium residents are oriented toward the substrate, they rarely sport the delicate barbels that give "cats" their popular name. You must use rounded, small-grain gravel or sand. Avoid sharply edged or glass-based substrates that could erode or wear away barbels. Additionally, provide a fine-grained bottom so that falling food does not disappear (and decompose) between stones. Remember that many popular cats like to sift sand, so choose the grain size accordingly. The size of the gravel should permit catfish to engage in their natural behavior.

Gravel colors: When we consider elements like gravel, we move into the area of decoration. A choice of decor is personal, but there are some helpful basic principles to consider. Fluorescent colors may be a popular style, but they do overpower the colors of fish. White gravel will usually cause aquarium fish to tone down their colors, as the natural reflex is to blend in to avoid predation. A darker-colored substrate will do the opposite, generally bringing out the ornate markings found on the flanks of many *Corydoras* and *Loricariid* species.

Aquarium backing: The same general principles apply to the aquarium backing. Painting the outside back of the aquarium with acrylic craft paint is a trick used by many, as is the purchase of commercially produced three-dimensional or glossy paper backing. Blue, gray, black, or green tones predominate in the choices offered. Bright or pale colors will either overpower or bleach out fish colors. All aquariums look better with a backing, as looking through the clear glass at the living room wallpaper decorated with electrical wires and filter hoses is not the effect most aim for. However, decorating an aquarium back once the tank is up and running is difficult.

Rocks: Aquarium keepers commonly collect or purchase rocks to decorate their tanks. A quick study of the properties of rocks can be helpful, as many will slowly leach minerals into the tank, hardening the water. This can be desirable in some cases and highly unwanted in others.

For those with a strong interest in keeping catfish in natural looking settings, it can help to remember that in nature, stream and river bottoms tend toward uniformity of colors. In an Amazonian habitat, it is rare to have rocks of different colors jumbled together.

Setting Up

A catfish aquarium is a simple, interconnected system. It starts outside of the water. The tank should be placed on a stable, strong, sturdy, and attractive stand. One gallon (4 L) of water weighs approximately 8 pounds (4 kg), which makes even a 20-gallon (75 L) tank into a serious weight. Only the largest aquariums can be a problem for poorly constructed floors, but even smaller aquariums can be too much for some tables or bookcases.

A wide variety of aquarium stands can be found in any aquarium store. Make certain the stand is solid, as a water-filled aquarium should never wobble. A tank that moves can quickly become a danger, as uneven stress on the silicone that holds it together can result in the failure of that silicone. The resulting floods are messy, disheartening, and very expensive. Silicone tanks are strong and reliable structures if their limits are respected. Never move a tank with water in it, and make certain tanks are placed onto level surfaces. Many fish keepers will add insurance by putting Styrofoam sheets or strips of foam-backed carpeting under their tanks to help absorb any unevenness under the glass. If one considers the weight of an aquarium, a simple piece of gravel between the stand and the bottom of the tank can become an enormous force capable of fracturing even the best-quality glass.

The next item needed is a comfortable chair from which you can relax and watch your fishes. Aquarium placement can be a key to success, as an out-of-the-way tank you glance at once a day is not likely to thrive. The tank should be in a quiet place that makes routine observation of fish relaxing and comfortable.

Fish are very sensitive to vibrations passing through their water, so a hallway, corridor, or busy family room may not be the best option. Catfish are among the least skittish fish we can keep, but that calm should not cause them to be placed in stressful locations.

Set up your aquarium close to an electrical outlet to avoid dangerous jungles of wires.

Also carefully consider where your tank will be in relation to your doors and windows. Although catfish do not usually change much in sunlight, many of their tank mates will look very good in natural light. The problem comes when the aquarist cannot see any fish because of algae growing on the glass. Algae-eating cats will not remove everything. Constantly scraping algae off the glass is a discouraging chore, almost as discouraging as the scratches on the glass that go with it. Diffused sunlight in a bright room is not going to give your tank problems, although many aquarists like to keep their tank in areas where only the lights in the hood illuminate the aquarium.

Controlling the heat in an aquarium during winter can be a problem in a poorly located aquarium. Do not put an aquarium stand above a home-heating vent or system, as in some rare cases it can throw the aquarium heater's thermostat off. The same problem can be caused by placing the tank where it will receive direct blasts of cold air from a door opening to the elements.

Household chemicals can be problematic for all fish tanks. Kitchens or bathrooms are bad locations due to cooking or chemical residues forming a scum on the surface of the water. You should be careful about using household sprays, hairsprays, insecticides, soaps, cleaners, or chemicals where they can settle on the water surface. A surprising danger can be the careless use of ammonia-based glass cleaners on aquariums. Ammonia is a deadly poison to fish.

Basic Maintenance

All the equipment available on the market simply buys time. Dirty water quickly leads to dead fish. Maintaining the quality of the water and the cleanliness of a captive catfish habitat involves a small amount of good, old-fashioned work. An aquarium in which the water is never changed but heavy filtration is used may look clean. The water may be clear. However, unseen toxins will build up. Contrary to the expectations of many new fish keepers, a fair percentage of the catfish in the hobby are very sensitive to water pollution. Luckily, the solution is easy.

The best regimen is to change regularly at least 25 percent of the water in the tank weekly. In a lightly stocked tank, water changes can wait a little longer. However, creating a predictable routine and sticking with it is much easier. For some reason, many people who happily take ten minutes every morning to water the plants will forget to put aside twenty minutes a week to care for their fishes. A

The day's catch on the Rio Orinoco.

Lithoxancistrus tigris L275, the Okapi plecostomus.

neglected tank quickly becomes a big cleaning job, and for the enjoyment of any hobby, hard work should be avoided.

There is a debate about how much water should be changed. Ideally, larger water changes would seem better, but that works only if you have a pristine supply of water. Most fish keepers have to deal with chemically treated water. If your water supply is treated with chlorine, pet shop dechlorination products will effectively neutralize this chemical, which is very injurious to fish. However, it is increasingly common for municipal treatment plants to use chloramine. This water treatment chemical is more stable and longer acting than chlorine and therefore very effective for drinking water. Some aquarium trade water treatment products will break the chemical bond in chloramine causing a quick release of toxic ammonia. On a very large-scale water change, this release can kill your fish, usually by burning their respiratory systems. You can consult with knowledgeable staff at a good aquarium shop to find which neutralizers are both effective and available in your region for this problem. However, changing a quarter of the tank's volume generally allows for a balance in which your fish will prosper.

To change water, you need a siphon hose and possibly a large bucket (for a 20-gallon [75-L] or larger tank, a 5-gallon [20-L] food-grade bucket is easiest). To start the siphon without using your mouth, submerge a 3-foot (1-m) length in the water until it is filled. Cap one end with your thumb and draw it out of the tank, not releasing your thumb until the submerged end is higher than the outlet end.

The water will flow freely. Remember that 1 gallon (4 L) of water weighs approximately 8 pounds (4 kg). Filling a 5-gallon (20-L) bucket to the top can make aquarium maintenance into a painful chore!

A useful option is a commercial water-changing system. For aquarists who do not double as weight lifters, they are well worth the small investment they demand. These systems use a swimming pool or water bed-type suction valve that attaches directly to a faucet. The direction of the flow is easily controlled. The aquarist simply has to attach the device and watch closely as it removes the desired percentage of tank water and then make a simple adjustment to have it refill the aquarium.

These systems, and many simple siphon hoses, should have a gravel vacuum tube attached at the intake end. Follow the instructions to remove easily (via the suction used for the routine water change) any debris, uneaten food, or fish wastes that have settled on the bottom.

The next task is to care for the aquarium's glass. An aquarium is a living system that does not always do the expected. At times, you will face algae blooms, generally if you overfeed, overilluminate, or have the tank in a location where it receives direct sunlight. The glass can be wiped weekly with a nontoxic sponge. Soaps should never be in contact with the inside of an aquarium as any detergent will strip the protective slime coating from fish, severely compromising their immune systems. If you leave the algae-cleaning chore too long, the glass will have to be scraped. Be careful to avoid creating unsightly and permanent scratches.

Plants will have to be pruned. Fluorescent tubes need checking. Although they will light up for several years, after about six months, they no longer provide a full light spectrum to aid the growth of plants. This is also the time to clean your filter, if necessary.

Plants

Aquarium catfish are such a diverse group that generalizations become difficult. Many an aquarist has been surprised to learn that his or her new vegetarian catfish is resourceful enough to forage on its own and will not only control algae but decimate the plants it grows on. Other cats prove to be ideal inhabitants for heavily planted aquariums. The only way to be certain of what you are getting is to look at the species description section in the second half of this manual, where plant-eating catfish will be specifically identified.

To complicate matters (and make them infinitely more interesting), plants have their own complex needs. The new fish keeper who buys an expensive and beautiful *Cabomba* plant only to have it rapidly dissolve into an unsightly mess is on the verge of a fun set of discoveries. The important thing is not to decide that plants are impossible to keep or that an aquatic green thumb is an inborn thing. Some plants are even more difficult to keep than fish.

The decision on which plants are best for an aquarium is similar to the one that must be made in choosing fish. There are two major directions. Either the aquarist will choose plants that will adapt to local conditions, or the aquarist will adapt to the conditions the plants call for. The ability for informed compromise may be the key to an aquatic green thumb. Looking at the conditions at hand can be the first step.

Lighting is key.

The average store-bought aquarium hood will offer enough illumination for the aquatic version of shade plants. While limiting, this still

A Cryptocoryne *plant.*

leaves a wide range of beautiful possibilities. However, plants that grow well at lower levels of light are harder to find in shops than the quick growing species favored by the aquatic plant trade. Low-light needs often correlate with slow growth, which makes these plants more expensive. Large-scale aquatic plant farms naturally prefer species that are productive in brightly lit, open ponds. This creates a catch-22, as most plants in the average store will not last long under the lighting most fish keepers have to offer. This is the origin of the myth that real aquarium plants are tough to keep and discourages the average hobbyist from creating the kind of easily maintained aquatic garden sometimes seen in books like this. If we assume most aquarists will be using fluorescent systems, then either specialized or homemade hoods will be needed for difficult plants. Tubes added to the system will increase success with all plants and allow the keeping of more demanding species.

Along with lighting comes motivation. All the equipment in the world will not take the place of routine gardening. Fast growing, bright-light plants need pruning, replanting, and fertilizing. An individual who enjoys puttering with the summertime flowers can delight in an indoor, year-round aquatic garden. However, a person with no interest in gardens or a distaste for gardening routines should focus on the group of plants that will be presented first.

Standard-Light, Low-Maintenance Aquarium Plants

Most low-light aquarium plants come, as we might expect, from the shaded areas of the tropical forest. Their habitats are generally shallow. They may live partially or totally above

water for part of the year. In the aquarium, they generally thrive under standard fluorescent hood lighting.

Java fern (*Microsorium pteropus*) is a strange and fascinating plant. It has a tendency to flourish for some and be impossible for others. With a moderate current and subdued lighting, the lovely leaves of the Java fern will grow quite large, and plantlets will break off from their tips. Java ferns should be attached to rocks or driftwood, as they do poorly (often dying) if their

An Amazon sword.

roots are buried. They seemingly have the ability to die, and yet suddenly reappear even months later when conditions are to their liking.

Larger specimens are excellent candidates for the back of poor to moderately illuminated aquariums.

Asia offers us a diverse group of low-light species grouped in the genus *Cryptocoryne.* Identifying the different species available can be tricky. They are sporadically available in better-supplied pet stores, usually at a higher price than the more common (and harder to grow) bunch plants. Aquarists should purchase three or four "crypts" to start with, as if they do establish themselves in a tank, they are rewarding to keep. They do not need a lot of light, and some will grow leaves right to the surface. The red-toned species are especially attractive. They are also an unexpected bonus for those decorating their tanks, as generally red-toned bunch plants need intense lighting.

Asian *Cryptocoryne* may not be natural in a tank of South American fish. However, small cats like the popular *Corydoras* love to sit in the shade of their leaves. As is the case with all slow-growing plants, their tough leaves are not too appealing to herbivorous *Loricariids.* Some catfish will, however, amuse themselves by digging up *Cryptocorynes.*

Africa brings us the lovely, if sometimes hard to locate, *Bolbitis heudelotii* fern. This plant can be very expensive, as it is a very slow-growing species. *Bolbitis* will become very tall and are extremely beautiful and hardy. Its needs are similar to those of the Java fern, however, it seems to do best in a slight current. One small piece can, over several years, cover the entire back of even a large tank, but patience is needed. Since it must be tied to a rock or piece of driftwood rather than planted, few catfish find any more interest in *Bolbitis* than as a platform for algae.

A number of *Anubias* species are found in Africa. *Anubias nana* is another low-light possibility, though it will thrive in brighter tanks as well. Like *Bolbitis,* this lovely little broad-leaved species must be attached to rocks or driftwood, with water circulation around its roots. All *Anubias* take some looking for, although the Internet has rendered them much more accessible. Generally, they call for great patience because they are sold in small cuttings and are not rapid growers, but they are well worth waiting for.

Java moss: A plant well loved by fish breeders, the java moss *(Vesicularia dubyana)* may be the easiest low-light plant in the hobby. It will sometimes prosper even in unlit tanks, as long as they are situated in well-lit rooms. This moss will form complex carpets if attached to rocks and driftwood and will even spread out and attach itself to the gravel on the bottom. Masses of this plant will reach the surface in shallow tanks, often making it hard to see your fish.

Java moss provides an excellent environment for small life-forms. It will support rich colonies of microscopic life, providing excellent food for catfish fry. *Corydoras* and *Aspidoras* will scatter their eggs in this moss. In single-species tanks, young will often grow up in the moss with very little special attention from their keepers.

On the downside, java moss is a pest in tanks with power filters. Pieces break off and clog filter intakes. Since such filters will also remove fry from tanks, they are best for nonbreeding show tanks anyway. Java moss is the secret ingredient in many a sponge-, air-, or under-gravel-filtered breeding aquarium.

Vallisneria and Sagittaria sp. (and there are several possibilities) are a completely different class of plants. These are aquatic grasses, successful in many different environments. They love bright light but will prosper at a much more restrained level under a standard hood. Like *Cryptocoryne*, they spread by sending runners under the sand or gravel. The taller species are lovely at the back of a tank. *Farlowella* and *Sturisoma* cats love to perch on the taller species.

Standard-Light, High-Maintenance Plants

Some plants prefer bright lighting but can grow slowly in low-light situations. Although the plants we have just looked at can more or less be put in the tank and left to grow, the next few need more attention. These are cutting plants and are commonly available at very reasonable prices in any well-equipped aquarium store. Watch for specimens with their roots already in place.

Hygrophila species are in this group. These bright green beauties behave like trees, in that they tend to bunch their foliage near their tops. If treated like a miniature terrestrial hedge and continually trimmed, this "stalkiness" in *Hygrophila* can be avoided.

Water wisteria *(Hygrophila difformis)* is a bit of an exception to the rules about the group, as it can float or be rooted. It is a hit-or-miss plant, either growing at a prodigious rate, or disappearing with equal speed, depending upon the water in which it is kept.

Echinodorus, the Amazon swords, can often do well if light gets to the bottom of the tank. They do best for those who use an easily available aquarium plant fertilizer.

Bacopa caroliniana can be a difficult species for some and easy for others. It reacts very well to old-fashioned incandescent hoods but needs more intense fluorescent lighting than the standard aquarium hood offers. If you are lucky, stalks can emerge through openings in the hood and produce delicate flowers.

Standard-Light Floating Plants

In the catfish hobby, floating plants do not have the importance they do for other species of egg-laying fishes. However, they are quite useful for creating floating meadow type habitat tanks. Duckweed *(Lemna minor)* will grow anywhere, to the point where it is a pest. It is a disaster in power filter set-ups, where it clogs the intakes. Hornwort *(Ceratophyllum demersum)* is an attractive floater that dissolves with startling speed when unhappy (creating quite a mess) but that can be an ideal beginner's plant if it likes the conditions offered.

Light-Loving Plants

Light-loving plants need more technical support. Keepers of these beauties will often install carbon dioxide (CO_2) injection systems, nonstandard hoods, and mixed types of lighting. These plants can easily demand more energy than the fish swimming around them.

Commonly available species include *Cabomba* sp., *Ludwigia* sp., the red or pink forms of *Hygrophila,* and a host of commonly but sporadically available cutting or bunch plants. Beware though. Fast-growing plants often have delicate leaves. As you will soon see, aquascaping with soft-leaved plants in a *Loricariid* cat habitat would be like decorating a rabbit hutch with lettuce plants. The slow growers with their heavy, unpalatable leaves are generally a better choice for these catfish.

Although they arrived in the hobby sold as scavengers, most catfish need more attention to their diets than other aquarium residents. The old attitude that cats are eaters of leftovers and garbage has taken decades to die, and thousands of catfish have died because of it.

Catfish have varied needs. There are carnivorous, omnivorous and herbivorous species. Since the latter poses the greatest puzzle to beginners, we will start with the vegetarians.

Herbivores

Herbivores eat a lot, and produce a lot of waste. This is not surprising since they are sold as algae eaters and usually do a good job on that pest. However, no healthy aquarium can produce enough algae for it to be counted on as a staple food.

As catfish popularity has boomed, the aquarium industry has taken notice. There are now very high-quality, intensively researched sinking pellet and wafer foods designed specifically for bottom dwellers.

For do-it-yourself types, softened garden vegetables are an appealing and healthy possibility. By parboiling or freezing thin zucchini slices, pesticide-free spinach, or romaine lettuce leaves, aquarists can provide first-rate nutrition to all herbivorous plecos. Lightly boiled potato or zucchini, frozen peas, or carrot rounds are also popular options that can be frozen and fed as needed. All of the vegetable foods are excellent for both adults and fry, although they will call for a bit more preparation and possibly cleaning up than the processed commercial options. Preparing a month's catfish food all at once takes much less time than does caring for a dog or cat in one day. Many fish keepers delight in watching the energy with which sucker mouths will attack a slice of zucchini.

Omnivores and Carnivores

Omnivores and carnivores are as easy as any other tropical fish to feed. They too need varied and good-quality nutrition. They also need their keepers to keep a sharp eye on how much food actually gets to them. Aggressive and fast swimming midwater-dwelling fish will often eat all the food before catfish even have a chance to see it. You may have to feed your fish in two stages, as simply dumping in extra food will cause pollution problems.

Commercial flake and pellet foods are a good option as a staple diet for catfish in communities, if not for the delicate species. Fish keepers may have to experiment with newly imported animals, as they may turn up their noses at one manufacturer's food and devour another's product

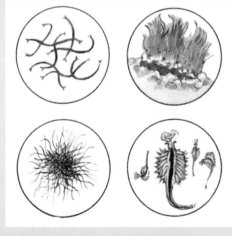

The bottom-feeding habits of Corydoras *species assure that live foods not consumed by other aquarium residents will not escape these efficient scavengers. Clockwise from top left: bloodworms, algae, brine shrimp, and tubifex worms. Other readily taken live foods include white worms, daphnia, and mosquito larvae.*

for no apparent or easy-to-identify reason. For variety or for fish that will not take flakes, high-quality frozen foods can be fed.

Bloodworm is a commonly available option for hobbyists who have no allergic reaction to the proteins in these frozen insect larvae. Should you experience even the slightest reaction to bloodworms, you should immediately and permanently discontinue their use. Their convenience is far outweighed by the dangers of an allergic reaction. Frozen brine shrimp is the other easy-to-locate option. Enterprising aquarists can also find many recipes for homemade seafood-based concoctions on the Internet.

Nocturnal cats will not always adjust their feeding strategies to daylight feeding times. It is always best to offer them some food soon after the lights go out.

Live Food

Live food, while it may sound disturbing, is useful for maintaining catfish in good condition and preparing them for breeding. *Corydoras* love worms. White worms (and the smaller grindal worm) can be easily cultured in a cool basement or an old fridge. Starter cultures with instructions are easy to track down on the Internet or in aquarium clubs. Catfish food can also be captured by finding a natural daphnia (water flea) pond. Such foods can often be a spawning trigger for small species. Earthworms, if from a source where lawn chemicals and pesticides are not present, can be chopped up and fed fresh to all catfish.

It is possible to purchase the cysts of brine shrimp (*Artemia* sp.) at pet stores and from the Internet. This is a superb food for small catfish and for fry. Most of these cysts have traditionally come from Utah. However, poor harvests over several years recently created a market for brine shrimp cysts from Russia and several

Many dry prepared foods are available for the aquarium hobbyist. Not every formulation is right for catfish species, so the hobbyist should do some research to make the right choices. As with any well-maintained aquarium, care should always be taken to avoid overfeeding.

northern countries in Asia. All need saltwater, though the level of salinity will vary from source to source. They usually hatch in aerated water 24 to 48 hours after introduction. Check with the supplier for details and methods for the type purchased. The short time needed to learn how to raise this food is more than compensated for by the excellent effect it can have on your fish.

Nontraditional Food

Some catfish fry (i.e., *Corydoras pygmaeus*) are too small for traditional foods. Often, they can find some nutrition in the microorganisms found on healthy clumps of java moss or even in some types of algae, but this will not suffice for large numbers of fry. Laboratory supply sources can provide breeders with starter cultures for microscopic foods, and the Internet or an aquarium club can lead aquarists to a source of microworms. This tiny food is simple to culture and very useful for the fry of most species and types of tropical fish.

BREEDING CATFISH

Why go to all the trouble of getting catfish to reproduce when they can be bought at the local petshop? The decision to try breeding catfish usually revolves around simple curiosity and the desire to learn.

Why Breed Catfish?

Raising aquarium fish fry is one of the more intriguing aspects of the hobby. It calls for skill, research, and attention to detail—all of which add up to a pleasant challenge for most fish keepers. It is fun to do. There can also be an economic incentive, as young catfish of all species can always find a home.

In the case of uncommon species, there is no guarantee they will ever be encountered again. Many "L" plecos or *Corydoras* are imported two or three times but may come from regions where they are among the few commercially interesting species. Once collectors find easier fishing grounds, the fish are effectively lost to the hobby. If no one has begun to produce captive-bred specimens, these attractive and interesting species can, in hobby terms, become little more than photos in books like this.

Breeding rarities is especially satisfying when a breeder is able to observe catfish doing

The African **Chiloglanis** *species look much like* **plecostomus.**

something unexpected and therefore add to our collective knowledge of these animals. However, there is no need to be the first to have or reproduce a species, as even the common cats are fun to spawn and raise.

How to do this is not a simple question to answer, as catfish are such a diverse group. Most of the hobbyist-produced catfish in the aquarium world originate in South America. While information on Lake Tanganyika's cuckoo cat can be found in the species description section, most successes have been with Amazonian animals. Strategies for four representative cats appear below. If they do not offer deep details on specific animals an aquarist may wish to try, they will at least point to directions that can be taken in experimenting.

Breeding Corydoras

Corys are often bred in the home aquarium, although some species have stumped even the experts. These fish pose an interesting puzzle. They will often spawn easily, even in the home aquarium, but can be difficult to raise in quantities. Breeding corys calls first and foremost for preparation. Any leftover ideas of corys as garbage cleaners will vanish once an aquarist has seen how important cleanliness is to the successful reproduction of these animals.

A common trick for breeding a cat like *Corydoras aeneus* or *C. paleatus* is to separate the sexes and start feeding the fish a protein-rich diet. Frozen or live food can be used. High-quality flakes or pellets may work, but in general, it is advisable to go for the best-quality foods at this time. You will be rewarded by seeing the females rapidly fill with eggs.

Sterilize the breeding tank, largely to remove any snails, and put the corys into shallow water of the same chemistry and temperature they are used to. Many aquarists will add boiled acrylic yarn mops or clean plants to the tank, and aeration is necessary. Once the fish have settled in, prepare some cooler, dechlorinated water. Turn off the heater and remove some tank water, replacing it with much cooler water of the same composition. With some more difficult species, you can use rain, reverse osmosis, or demineralized water to simulate a tropical rainstorm.

Most of the time, properly conditioned *Corydoras aeneus* will spawn soon after the onrush of cool water. You may, however, have to repeat the process several times, and some species will wait until the temperature goes back up again to spawn. There are variations with each species in the group and often with each group of individuals. For uncooperative groups (the breeding group should have at least two males for every female), there are a few possible tricks. You can go back to conditioning the potential breeders. If they are available, try adding a few new individuals to the group, to shake up the social

structure. As an alternative, if you have other species spawning, throw in a bit of their water to see if the chemicals in it stimulate your reluctant corys.

With pygmy corys (*C. pygmaeus, C. hastatus* and *C. habrosus*), it can be even easier. In a snail-free, single-species tank full of java moss, large groups of these active and hardy fish will spawn after a cooling water change. Fry will often reach adulthood with the original school, provided water quality is kept high and small food is offered.

Often, freshwater will be greeted by an explosion of activity but not necessarily spawning. Cory egg laying is an involved process. Females will be chased by males, and the couple (or trio) will repeatedly adopt a position in the shape of the letter "T." Theories abound as to how the eggs are actually exposed to sperm. However, what we do know is the female carries the eggs, depositing them onto a chosen substrate. The process can take some time and can result in anywhere from a very few to around a hundred eggs.

Most corys will produce fairly large adhesive eggs. These will be in the acrylic mop or on easily removed leaves, if the female has accidentally cooperated with the hobbyist, or all over the glass if she has not. Adults or eggs should be removed for maximum success. The eggs can be gently scraped off their surface (many use a clean razor blade to break the sticky bond) and moved to a smaller container of clean, chemical-free water. With an air stone and enough methylene blue to stain the water without rendering the eggs invisible, the eggs are incubated for five to six days. The eggs are delicate and should be watched for fungus. Infertile eggs should be removed immediately before fungus can spread

Corydoras spawning behavior.

to good eggs. Changing the incubation water frequently is a good idea.

The fry swim approximately two days after hatching. They are very sensitive to pollution and yet need a lot of nutritious food (freshly hatched brine shrimp is a favorite). Frequent water changes are the order of the day. As they grow, they can be moved to larger, and deeper, grow-out aquariums.

Breeding Bristlenoses

Ancistrus, or bristlenose catfish, are often easier to breed than they are to identify. To start, you have to recognize their territorial natures. You can keep one male with several females. A good trick is to place a flat rock (slate is good) on the bottom of the tank, and place a clay flowerpot with a door knocked out of the side onto it. Place it so you can see into it. The male will sit in his doorway, waiting for females to visit him. Because of his armor and his ability to handle himself, this breeding setup can even be in a community tank with cichlids.

Bristlenose eggs are deposited onto the walls of the cave. After spawning, the female wanders off, no longer concerned by the process. In too-small a tank, she should be removed, as the male will attack her should she been seen as threatening the brood. The male guards the large, bright orange eggs, and he does it well. After four to five days, he even helps the fry break out of their shells.

The second phase features a wriggling mass of larvae hanging on the wall, under the watchful eye of the male. In a community,

you should steal the poorly developed fry at this point. After about two days, they will burst out of the nest and rush for the surface, no longer under the protection of the male. Given that at this stage bristlenose fry have enormous, rich, bright orange yolk sacs attached to their bellies, they have little chance of survival in an aquarium.

The young devour soft vegetable food and wafers, and they appreciate some freshly hatched brine shrimp. This food rapidly fouls the water. *Ancistrus* young have little resistance to bacterial disease or tolerance for pollution. Frequent heavy-water changes are called for. The young grow rapidly and are always in demand.

Breeding Zebra Cats

Surprisingly few of the "L" type, *Loricariid* cats are spawned and raised by hobbyists. This may flow from the fact *Loricariid* breeding strategies are often secretive and finding spawning triggers can be hard. For most of these fish, keepers have to be prepared to use a large tank for a single species, which, if things go well, they will not see much of.

Many Otocinclus are found in floating meadows like this.

A tiny **Parotocinclus** *spec. from Peru.*

right: **Albino** *Ancistrus munching on zucchini.*

below: **Rynchodoras xingui** *is built to suck insect larvae from crevices.*

Predictably, the pastime of breeding L-cats has not caught on. However, when the zebra pleco hit our shores, many aquarists wanted lots of these expensive gems. They have become the most commonly spawned aquarium *Loricariid* for the simple reason that they are the one the most hobbyists have invested time and energy into.

The tricks used for this species are generally applicable for most Rio Xingu/Rio Tapajos suckermouths. A number of these fish have had reported spawns in captivity (L-28, 34, 38, 46, 66, 70, 89, 129, 134, 144, 147, 159, 182, 201, 260, 262, 270, LDA 08, and LDA 05) at the time this manual was written, so the project is very possible. We can take the technique for *Hypancistrus zebra* as a template to experiment with the others.

Start with a tank of around 30 gallons (115 L), filled with slightly acidic, soft, clean water at a temperature of 84°F to 86°F (28.9°C to 30.0°C). Success may be had with moderately hard and alkaline water, but soft water is a big part of their natural habitat. Excellent quality, fast flowing filtration is essential. Adding

power heads simply to push water can be a good idea. Make sure the flow from all devices goes in the same direction.

The bottom can be bare or dusted with a thin layer of fine sand. The decor has to include rocks and stable caves, angled so the filter outflow goes through them. Some aquarists will cut short lengths of 1-inch (2.5 cm) diameter pvc pipe. These "caves" have the advantage of being easily cleaned, inspected, and moved.

An air pump connected to large air stones or bars helps to produce as much oxygenation in this water as possible. Add three pairs of zebra plecos, and watch them sort out territories. If males become very aggressive during feeding, start looking into the pipes. At one point, a male should tolerate a female approaching, and eventually entering, his chosen cave. She will leave after spawning (make certain she has somewhere to go) while the male guards the eggs, *Ancistrus* style. He will protect the brood until it is free-swimming.

Adults and young will need a nourishing diet of live daphnia or blackworms, or of frozen bloodworms and brine shrimps. If the fish have spawned in a zebra-only tank, the young should be able to grow up with their parents. Watch water quality and feeding. In a short period, the tank will have a thriving colony of zebras or of the other smaller suckermouths that can be bred under the same conditions.

Breeding Sturisoma, the Royal Farlowella Catfish

All *Farlowella* are fun fish to breed because of their interesting brood care. The problem for hobbyists is finding spawning triggers. *Farlowella* breed when they want to, which can be trying for the patience of keepers who dedicate an aquarium for their reproduction and then have to wait for long periods of time with no control over events. The closely related *Sturisoma festivum*, which is even sold as the royal farlowella, is a much more cooperative catfish. It is harder to find but extraordinarily interesting.

Breeding the royal farlowella requires tanks of at least 30 gallons (115 L) mostly because the gentle adults are over 8 inches (20 cm) in length and have trouble navigating their rigid, sticklike bodies around small tanks. Armor that can save a life in the wild can be a limiting factor in the crowded safety of an aquarium.

The water should be soft and slightly acidic with a temperature in the high 70s°F (mid 20s°C). It is best to keep the fish alone if the plan is to raise a large number of young. If not, these *Sturisoma* spawn well in community tanks with peaceful tetras, dwarf cichlids, and *Corydoras*. As always, the slow, nocturnal *Sturisoma* must get enough food in the form of live black worms, mosquito larvae, and algae. As with most omnivorous cats, they will thrive on sliced potato, zucchini, and frozen peas.

Ideally, their tank should have several stands of tall plants like *Echinodorus* (Amazon sword) or *Vallisneria*. These are preferred spawning sites. Often, however, despite plenty of ideal sites, the parents will choose to spawn on the back glass of the aquarium. Around 100 to 150 eggs are laid and guarded by the male, who will have developed pronounced bristles at the side of his head. After about one week, the eggs hatch and the young immediately swim to the nearest plants or ornaments. Three days later, they will have used up their yolk sacs and begun to feed. The best way to feed the young is by attaching a romaine lettuce leaf to an air stone. The young are drawn to the current and begin feeding on the lettuce. They are sensitive to less-than-ideal water conditions, and great care must be taken to ensure the rearing tanks are kept clean. If not, the entire brood of apparently healthy, growing royal farlowella can be lost in a matter of an hour or two.

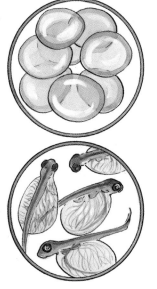

From eggs to larvae to free-swimming young.

Megalechis thoracata, *a worm eater.*

Baby **Sturisoma** *feeding on lettuce.*

Corydoras sterbai *clasping egg.*

Baby **Corydoras sterbai** *look different.*

Corydoras sterbai *is one of the most popular catfish.*

Catfish, with their body armor, are well protected against physical injury and by extension, against attacks by parasites. Armor is an advantage for catfish and their keepers, but it also makes diagnosing the common internal diseases extremely difficult. In effect, curing catfishes once a disease is established is hard. Therefore, their health is more dependent on prevention than treatment.

How the fish keeper maintains catfish depends on how he or she purchases. Start by finding a good retailer who takes pride in selling healthy fish that have been quarantined. Always take the time to study potential purchases carefully. The ideal situation is to observe any interesting catfish while they are eating. If the fish are behaving normally in the vendor's tanks and show a healthy appetite, they are likely in good health. Here are some tips for studying cats you may wish to buy.

Suckermouth Catfish

Ich is a serious problem with suckermouths. This parasite is very common in aquariums and attacks weakened or stressed fish. Once an epidemic breaks out (an all too likely scenario once this creature is chilled or is in the close confines of a new aquarium environment), large numbers of parasites will form white cysts on the skin of their hosts. They feed on the host's fluids and can be attacked only in their free-swimming stage, after the cysts burst and multitudes of parasites set out on a search for a new home.

Suckermouth armor plates prevent ich and other parasites from attacking plecos as quickly as other fish. This is an advantage. However, once the fish are infected, the parasite will usually not attack in visible or easily treated areas. Make sure any Loricariids bought are acting normally. The first places these parasites attack are the soft belly and the gills. Check the underside of the fish against the glass, and make sure there are no white spots or films on the skin. At this point, potential purchasers can also check for larger parasites—a much less likely danger. Fish that are abnormally placid and sit on the bottom fanning their pectoral and ventral fins often have their gills badly infected with ich. This is a common problem with the popular gold nugget plecos, among others. As a basic rule—never buy catfish that might be infected.

While checking for ich, look for velvet (oodinium), a white or yellow parasite that can, in some cases, be mistaken for ich. It tends to form patches and be much smaller than ich.

Bacterial disease first presents itself as red patches on the base of the paired fins on the underside of plecos, while internal parasites and irreversible starvation cause hollow, concave bellies. Do not make the error of thinking

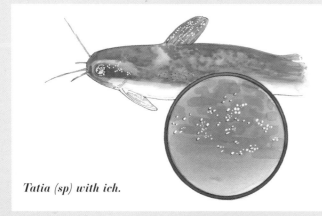

Tatia (sp) with ich.

you can easily cure such problems. By the time the catfish armor allows symptoms to show, it is unfortunately usually too late.

Armored Catfish

Armored catfish such as *Corydoras, Brochis,* and *Aspidoras* are hardy fish, to say the least. However, hemorrhagic bacterial disease can affect newly imported fish and will cause entire tankfuls of corys to die within hours. Never buy corys from tanks with dead animals, tanks where some animals have red zones near the posterior part of the body, or tanks where any individual fish have bleeding fins. This group of diseases is often brought on by shipping stress and is best avoided by buying corys at least one week after arrival at the store. Often, specimens subjected to the added stress of being taken home too soon will develop such infections while their tank mates at the store survive and regain their resistance.

Naked (Scaleless) Catfish

Naked (scaleless) catfish are a more difficult group. Here the soft skin is easily pierced by parasites and these fish are often the first to get sick in a tank. Check new acquisitions carefully. After the fish are brought home, check them carefully (they will often hide during the day) for the first 10 days to make sure that the stress of transfer has not brought on any disease. Ich is a common problem for *Pimelodus, Tatia, Synodontis* and especially glass catfish. The latter are also in that unfortunate class of fish known as "velvet magnets."

Often, when disease strikes your tank, your catfish will be last to get sick in the tank. Be vigilant and check your fish for signs of parasites on a regular basis. Ask your local store about recommended treatments.

A Loricariid with a sunken belly.

Maintaining Your Catfish

Once catfish are established in the home tank, disease becomes very rare. With adequate filtration, regular water changes, clean conditions, appropriate food, and nonaggressive tank mates, most catfish will outlive all their companion fish.

Fungus worries many new fish keepers, because it is such an obvious, hard-to-miss problem. Bear in mind that it is more of a secondary symptom than a disease. Often small plumes of fungus will infect the sharp spines of catfish if they have been handled carelessly or have been tangled in a net (always scoop catfish from the net with a cup). In most cases, fungus can be gently wiped away with a moist tissue, and the fish will recover without medication.

Make sure to keep up regular tank maintenance and check other fish carefully for signs of bacterial or parasitic outbreaks. With their defenses, your catfish are the furthest thing from a canary in a coal mine when it comes to spotting developing problems. It is their tank mates that must be counted on to provide obvious indications of disease.

Offering global suggestions for treatment options is very difficult. Antibiotics are increasingly difficult to get in aquarium stores, and aquarium medications are not standard from one region to another. Experienced local retailers will be the best resource if fish start to get sick.

SPECIES DESCRIPTIONS

This final chapter describes many catfish species. The fish keeper should continually refer to these pages when purchasing new specimens.

African Catfish

With the possible exception of Lake Tanganyika and Lake Malawi Cichlids, the intriguing tropical fish of Africa are largely ignored in the hobby. The fish-exporting industry outside of the Great Lakes of eastern Africa is not nearly as developed as it is in South America, the usual source of aquarium catfish. There are a number of African cats well worth the patience it may take to track them down. Finding them will show these catfish are not rare because they are unattractive.

In general, most African species are larger fish and can be ideal for community tanks with cichlids, especially species from their own continent. Mixing cichlids and cats usually works, but mixing across continents can be a very bad idea. Many African cichlids tend to bite the eyes out of South American plecos and even

The banks of the Amazon River near Iquitos, Peru.

Corydoras. Besides, the hard alkaline water necessary for African Lake cichlids is less than ideal for the South American catfish

African catfish are exported from two major areas. None of the species are produced commercially, at least in large numbers. The greatest number of species come from the Democratic Republic of Congo (formerly Zaire) where many suitable aquarium species are found along the Congo River. The second largest group is exported from Nigeria, where many exporters are located. The countries of Guinea, Cameroon, and Ghana export some aquarium fishes but only in small, not very significant numbers. An equally small group is also exported from Lake Tanganyika and Lake Malawi, where cats may come as side catches in the lucrative cichlid trade.

Whatever the source, African catfish are scaleless fish, making them more susceptible to ectoparasites such as ich. All new fish should be careful checked before purchasing them and quarantined when brought home.

Mochokidae, the Genus Synodontis

The feather barbed catfish are a widespread group with more than 100 described species ranging from less than 3 inches (8 cm) to over 18 inches (46 cm) in total length. They are hardy, mostly nocturnal fishes that will accept all foods offered. They prefer insect food such as mosquito larvae and bloodworms. While they are not true predators, they may eat smaller fishes at night, so they should not be kept with species significantly smaller than them. All *Synodontis* aquariums should have a good current and excellent filtration. A large-volume water change of 30 percent every two weeks will keep these hardy fish healthy.

All *Synodontis* have powerful and sharp spines on their dorsal and pectoral fins. They must be handled with great caution and, if possible, with gloves.

Most *Synodontis* species are rarely bred in the aquarium without the use of hormones, with the exception of two species found in Lake Tanganyika. In general, female *Synodontis* are heavier bodied and males are more slender. With many species, males are also more intricately patterned, with a greater number of spots or stripes.

When keeping the catfish of the Great Lakes, water conditions must be kept in mind. Nearly all popular aquarium catfish come from soft, pH neutral, or acidic waters. The water conditions in the Great Lakes are alkaline and hard. Lake Tanganyika catfishes should be kept at pH values above 8 in very hard water, as they adapt poorly to softer, more acidic, or neutral conditions.

Synodontis multipunctatus
(Boulenger 1898)
Cuckoo catfish.
Lake Tanganyika, East Africa
To 6 inches (15 cm)

S. multipunctatus is one of the most recognizable catfish to the cichlid hobbyist. They are found throughout coastal waters of Lake Tanganyika. Their small size of less than 6 inches (15 cm) and active schooling nature makes them ideal for sharing tanks with cichlids from their home lake. They are also the most easy to breed African catfish, and their breeding strategy is among the most interesting of all aquarium fishes. A school of these active swimmers is a fantastic sight in larger cichlid aquariums.

S. multipunctatus are brood parasites. They take advantage of the common cichlid broodcare strategy of mouthbrooding, in which these superbly adapted animals use their mouths as mobile nests for eggs, and in some species, even for fry. When mouthbrooding cichlids (in nature the most common hosts are *Ctenochromis horei*) spawn, the quick and opportunistic *Synodontis* will disturb the cichlids' activity, eating some of the cichlid eggs in the process and laying their own to replace them. The confused cichlid female picks up the small catfish eggs along with some of her own after each attack. When the targeted cichlids resume spawning, the catfish strike again and again, until the cichlid has picked up to 30 of the catfish eggs. Female mouthbrooding cichlids then carry the catfish eggs in the safety of their mouths, along with their own. The *Synodontis* eggs are small and have only small yolk sacs—developing rapidly and hatching just 12 hours after spawning. Just four days later, the catfish fry begin to eat. The cichlid eggs, needing seven days to start hatching, are doomed. The tiny catfish eat eggs much larger than their bodies, developing rapidly. Once all the cichlid eggs are eaten, the voracious catfish young quickly cannibalize each other. When the cichlid releases the fry for the first time, expecting to have a brood of her own species, fully formed catfish fry escape from her mouth into the rocks. At this stage, the catfish fry have reached sizes of up to a half inch (1.3 cm).

In the aquarium, *S. multipunctatus* will breed readily with many host species. However, the mouthbrooding cichlids of Lake Tanganyika are more aware of the danger of *Synodontis* than are cichlids found in the other Great Lakes. Ideal hosts for any breeding attempts are the many Lake Victoria cichlid species or Lake Malawi's *Aulonocara* and *Pseudotropheus*. These cichlids spawn frequently and readily pick up catfish eggs. To raise larger numbers of fry, the female cichlid should be "stripped" of the eggs with both the catfish and cichlid broods placed into separate suspended strainers in a small aquarium with an air stone below. The catfish young eat even with their yolk sacs on and must be fed frequently with crushed flake or frozen foods. To make sure the catfish fry do not cannibalize each other, they should be separated as soon as possible. Once they have assumed the body shape of the parents and are completely black in color (the spots develop later), they can be housed together without any trouble. They can, at this point, be raised with equally sized cichlid fry.

Synodontis petricola

(Matthes 1959)
Lake Tanganyika, East Africa
3 inches (8 cm)

S. petricola are the smallest *Synodontis* from Lake Tanganyika. They are similar to *S. multi-*

punctatus but have been observed opportunistically laying eggs in the nests of *Lamprologine* cichlids. *S. petricola* are easily bred in species tanks with spawning sites in the form of large flowerpots placed upside down and filled with glass marbles to the halfway mark. After several weeks of good feeding and large water changes, the parents begin to chase each other

TIP

Buying African Catfishes

African catfish are scaleless, which gives them less defense against common aquarium parasitic diseases than most fish. Before purchasing, please make sure the fish are healthy. Curing parasites on these fish is not an easy job.

Carefully check that there are no white spots (ich parasites) on the skin or fins of any fish in the tank. If ich is present, do not give in to the temptation to ignore it.

As with all aquarium fish, make sure that the bellies are not sunken looking—ask to see your catfish eat. Beware of incurable internal parasites or fish that in transit have gone so long without food they cannot bounce back.

Check that the underside of the catfish has no red patches. Look on the belly and the base of the fins for this sign of bacterial infection.

The feathered barbels on the catfish should be intact and free of infection (whitish slime or fungus).

The eyes should be clear and not sunken.

Leptoglanis camerunensis, an African catfish.

and then spawn in the flowerpots. The parents are removed after spawning, and the fry are raised in the breeding tank. Despite their rapid development in their early stages, *Synodontis* fry grow slowly in the first year.

The species *S. dhonti* and *S. polli* are similar but rarely imported.

Synodontis granulosus

(Boulenger 1900)
Lake Tanganyika, East Africa
To 8 inches (20 cm)

The deep waters of Lake Tanganyika are the home of this much sought after catfish. This absolute rarity is included in this manual because of its almost legendary status among keepers of Lake Tanganyika aquariums. Despite its plain body color, it is among the most striking African catfishes. The contrasting black-and-white fins and day-active behavior are rare among *Synodontis*, which are mostly nocturnal. They are territorial and chase each other frequently, but these altercations rarely lead to injuries. The relatively small mouth means that smaller fish are not bothered. When this species can be found, they are ideal community fish for all cichlids from the African Rift Lakes. Like all *Synodontis*, they are easy to feed and will take any aquarium fish food or live food offered.

Unfortunately, fewer than 50 *S. granulosus* are caught each year in the deep waters mostly off the coast of Burundi in northern Lake Tanganyika, although the fish is found everywhere in the lake. The species is among the most expensive catfish in specialty stores and a much sought after prize for many cichlid hobbyists. To date, the species has not been bred in the aquarium.

Phractura sp., a fascinating African catfish.

Synodontis angelicus

(Schilthuis 1891)
Congo River
To 8 inches (20 cm)

Stanley Pool on the mighty Congo River is home to many popular *Synodontis* species. This much sought after *Synodontis* is a good community fish for larger fishes from the region such as *Distichodus* tetras, *Steatocranus* (buffalo head cichlids), *Hemichromis* (jewel cichlids), and *Mormyrids* (elephant nose fish). It is another *Synodontis* with a legendary status in the hobby, although this time it hails from the softer, acidic river waters of Central Africa. Wild adults may reach lengths over 8 inches (20 cm), although they usually stay much smaller in aquariums. They become territorial with sexual maturity. The attractive coloration may fade somewhat once adult size is reached. In the aquarium trade, juveniles of less than 2 inches (5 cm) are offered at often very high prices. Large numbers of them are still exported from the Congo, but more and more come from Eastern Europe where they are bred by hormone injections. The species will eat algae along with any aquarium food offered.

Synodontis decorus

(Boulenger 1899)
Congo River
To 10 inches (25 cm)

This is another big catfish commonly sold to the unsuspecting as a juvenile aquarium fish. *S. decorus* is a very peaceful species that can be kept with

The popular Synodontis multipunctatus.

smaller fishes. With age the species develops a long, soft extension on the dorsal spine.

Synodontis eupterus— the Featherfin Catfish

(Boulenger 1901)
Nigeria
6 inches (15 cm)

This hardy catfish is widespread in the Chad, Volta, and Niger River basins. Today it is the most commonly exported species (mostly from Nigeria) and has unfortunately replaced the smaller but much better tempered *S. nigriventris* as the upside down catfish of the trade. Adults attain lengths of over 6 inches (15 cm) and may be kept with most hardy cichlids, even those found in Central America. They are ideal clean-up fishes that can eat great quantities of food. After eating, they often develop enormous but temporarily distended bellies that appear as if they had swallowed a golf ball.

Synodontis flavitaeniatus
Synodontis brichardi
Synodontis schoutedeni

(Boulenger 1919), (Poll 1959), (David 1936).
Congo River
6 inches (15 cm)

All three of the above species are from the Congo River and reach lengths of around

Beware!

There are some catfish you should never buy. Babies or juveniles of these species are cute novelties often sold at unscrupulous pet stores. Adults usually end up being killed after they have destroyed their home aquariums.

Phractocephalus hemioliopterus—red-tail cat, 48 inches (120 cm)

Arius seemani—Columbian shark, 36 inches (90 cm)

Pangasius hypophthalmus (synonym: *P. sutchi*)—Iridescent shark, 36 inches.

Pangasius sanitwongsei—Parroon shark, 60 inches (150 cm)

Pseudoplatystoma tigrinum—Tiger shovelnose, 60 inches (150 cm)

Wallago leeri, attu.—Helicopter cat, 36 inches (90 cm)

6 inches (15 cm). They are among the smaller *Synodontis* species. All are ideal community tank fishes with large enough companions and can be kept in well-planted aquariums with Congo tetras and cichlids from the region.

Synodontis nigriventris—Upside-Down Catfish

(David 1936)
Central and West Africa
To 3 inches (8 cm)

The most famous African catfish is found in the Congo River of Central Africa. Political instability in the region has made the fish available only infrequently of late. Normally, upside-down catfish are caught by the thousands in the Stanley Pool area not far upstream from the Democratic Republic of Congo's capital Kinshasa. The peculiar swimming position of this largely nocturnal catfish has made it popular in the aquarium hobby. As a matter of fact, this species will right itself only to take food from the bottom of the aquarium but will remain upside down at all other times, an adaptation to the fishes' nocturnal feeding behavior on insect larvae off the surface. The upside-down catfish attains lengths of less than 3 inches (8 cm) and will not harm any other aquarium fish or plants. To keep the shy fish happy during the day, small flowerpots or half coconut shells should be added as daytime resting spots. It is the only riverine species reported to have been bred in the aquarium without the use of hormones. Spawning is said to occur in small caves or under thick plant cover, and the fry are protected by the parents for some time.

Other African Catfish

Microsynodontis batesii

(Boulenger 1903)
Central Africa
To 4 inches (10 cm)

This is a small catfish found in Gabon, Cameroon, and Congo. Adults are less than 4 inches (10 cm) and make ideal community fishes with the smaller African barbs and tetras. This shy species is active at night and must be fed after the lights are turned off. In heavily planted tanks with small community fish, they may come out during the day or at least at feeding time. Unfortunately, this species is a rarity in aquariums.

Schilbe intermedius— the Grass Cutter

(Rüppell 1832)
Widespread in Africa
To 12 inches (30 cm)

These are hardy schooling fish for cichlid communities, where they patrol the open water looking for food. Smaller fishes are often considered prey by adult grass cutters. For many years, small specimens of this catfish were common in stores, but they have fallen out of favor over recent years because of their predatory habits and tendency to uproot plants.

Lophiobagrus cyclurus

(Worthinton and Ricardo 1937)
Lake Tanganyika, East Africa
4 inches (10 cm)

This uncommon small catfish from Lake Tanganyika is a good community fish that can be kept with smaller Lake Tanganyika cichlids such as *Julidochromis* and *Lamprologus*. *Lophiobagrus* is bred frequently in small tanks where the eggs are guarded by the parents in a small cave. As a secretion from adults can poison other fishes in buckets, bags, and even small tanks under stress, the fish should be handled carefully.

Phyllonemus typus— the Feather Barbeled Catfish

(Boulenger 1906)
Lake Tanganyika, East Africa
To 4 inches (10 cm)

This shy, gray Lake Tanganyika catfish is easily identified by its two long barbels with wide, fleshy extensions. They are good community fish that can be kept with most small or medium-sized cichlids from the lake. *Phyllone-*

TIP

The Electric Catfish

Malapterurus electricus, the electric catfish, is capable of generating powerful electric pulses to stun prey or scare off predators. Adults of over 2 feet (60 cm) in length are tough and powerful fish that are suited only for the public aquarium. Electric catfish are widespread across West, Central, and East Africa. They are not recommended for the home aquarium, although they do sometimes find their way into the dangerous novelty side of the trade.

mus have been bred in the aquarium on several occasions. The species are mouthbrooders and both parents care for the eggs and young.

Eutropiellus buffei—the Debauwi Catfish, the African Catfish

(Gras 1960)
West and Central Africa
2 inches (5 cm)

This busy catfish, often misidentified as *E. debauwi,* is a bread-and-butter aquarium trade fish, even showing up in the pet sections of North American department stores. The Debauwi catfish act much like a schooling tetra. They live in large groups in small streams. In the aquarium they adapt well and make lively community fish in well-planted tanks. Unfortunately, they are very susceptible to ich and must be checked very carefully over the first few weeks after introduction. If these gregarious fish are

Synodontis petricola is a small catfish from Lake Tanganyika.

Phyllonemus typus from Lake Tanganyika.

kept in groups of less than five individuals they will not do well in the aquarium and often waste away mysteriously, one at a time.

Amphilius, Chiloglanis, Leptoglanis and Phractura Species

The above genera are found in streams of West and Central Africa. The group consists of many species of mostly small catfish well

Adult red-tail catfish—not something to try at home.

adapted to fast flowing water. While many are ideal community aquarium fish, they are not exported often. Part of their strange unpopularity may be that they are only rarely shown in books. While they all need clean, highly oxygenated water, they are easy to feed and very peaceful with even tiny tetras and killifish. Look for occasional imports of these interesting catfish in larger aquarium shops. Many rain forest species such as these prefer slightly cooler temperatures than most aquarium fish as they live their lives in the shade of streams under the forest canopy. They can be kept in the low 70s°F (mid 20s°C).

Asian Catfish

Although a large percentage of our aquarium fishes are from Asia, the number of small aquarium catfish from the region is relatively low compared with South America and even Africa. In addition, none of the small Asian catfish are bred commercially, so the hobby relies on occasional wild caught imports, mostly from India.

Chandramara chandramara, *an uncommon Asian species.*

Hara hara—the Moth Catfish
(Hamilton 1822)
India and Myanmar
2.5 inches (6 cm)

This catfish has the distinction of having a popular name even less interesting than its scientific name. Found in mountain streams, this tiny nocturnal fish is very peaceful and can be kept with all small barb or gourami species. *Hara* caught in higher elevations need cooler temperatures (in the low 60s°F [about 15°C]), but most specimens will tolerate temperatures in the low 70s°F (mid 20s°C). *Hara* must be fed separately at night and do not always accept dried foods. Live or frozen foods are suggested.

Kryptopterus minor—the Glass Catfish
(Roberts 1989)
Southeast Asia
3 inches (8 cm)

The glass catfish is the most popular Asian species. It is often found ill in pet shops, as it not only handles stress poorly but broadcasts

Hara hara, *the Asian moth catfish.*

Hara jerdoni—*an Asian rarity.*

any infirmity through its transparent body. Healthy, they are excellent warm-water community fishes that need to be kept only with very calm fish that are smaller than them. Adult glass catfish will grow to 3 inches (8 cm). The aquarium should have a strong current and plenty of open swimming room in the center for this shy, schooling fish. A healthy school of glass catfish is a spectacular sight, but is not always easy to maintain because the species is very sensitive to disease. While not the beginner's fish it is too often sold as, this is a great catfish for the experienced enthusiast.

Mystus vittatus—Indian Catfish

(Bloch 1794)

India, Bangladesh and Myanmar

To 8 inches (20 cm)

The Indian catfish is a genial aquarium inhabitant. Although very small fish are considered prey by this species, Indian catfish can be kept with the larger gouramis, barbs, and other fish from the region. *Mystus* are active swimmers reminiscent of the better known South American *Pimelodus* species.

Chandramara chandramara— the Hovering Catfish

(Hamilton 1822)

India and Bangladesh

2 inches (5 cm)

The hardy hovering catfish is found in slow moving waters. It is not commonly found in pet shops, in spite of its charm. They are ideal day-active catfish that travel through the aquarium in small troops looking for food along the bottom. Their ventral fins are in constant motion, making them look like dragonflies hovering in the water. Despite their drab coloration, their

=== TIP ===

Two Giant Tropical Catfish

Asia: The Mekong River is home to Asia's largest catfish. *Pangasius gigas* is one of the largest freshwater fish in the world. Said to reach lengths of up to 10 feet (3 m), the huge catfish live in deeper waters of the Mekong. The species is now protected. In spite of this, fish over 6 feet (2 m) in total length are rarely caught.

South America: The Amazon is home to several species of giant catfish. The Salton is one of many species that can grow over 6 feet (2 m) in length. *Brachyplatystoma filamentosum* is found in most of the Amazon and its major tributaries. As it is a popular food fish in the Amazon basin, truly giant specimens are becoming increasingly rare.

behavior makes them very interesting catfish for the barb or loach aquarium.

Pseudomystus siamensis—the Asian Bumblebee Catfish

(Regan 1913)

Mekong River Basin

5 to 6 inches (13 to 15 cm)

The Asian bumblebee catfish is a hardy species that will tolerate a wide variety of water conditions. Like their South American counterparts/namesakes, they are nocturnal fishes rarely seen during the day. While this species grows less than 6 inches (15 cm), they are surprisingly efficient predators that should be kept only with larger fish.

South American Catfish

Doradidae, Raphaels, and Related Catfish

While we usually buy raphael cats because of their attractive shape and markings, their appeal goes beyond that. They are among the toughest and most adaptable of all aquarium fish, capable of surviving in unfiltered and unheated aquariums. Their well-armored bodies allow them to approach aquarium life, and even larger, more aggressive fish, with well-founded confidence.

On the downside, raphaels may eat small community fish. They are also very much nocturnal. It is rare to see one during the day outside of feeding time. In nature, they can be found scavenging for food in the leaf litter of many types of rain forest habitats. At night, the shallows are alive with small troops of these catfish looking for worms and insect larvae. In the home aquarium, they will rule the darkness.

Catching and netting raphaels must be done with great care. The fish has sharp barbed spines on the pectoral fins, which can injure the keeper or cause the fish to become caught in the net. Often they get so badly entangled that the net has to be cut off around the spine. To avoid this, raphaels should be caught with a net and then scooped into a cup before being lifted from the water. Once out of the water, they make loud croaking noises that can startle predators and fish keepers alike.

In aquariums, they are hardy and can be kept with most medium-sized community fish, where they can live for up to 20 years. Raphael catfish are excellent cleaners that search the bottom for leftover scraps of food. While their

=== **TIP** ===

Handling and Catching Catfish

Many species of catfish, including *Corydoras, Synodontis* and *Doradiids,* have sharp and often barbed defensive spines that can cause serious or painful injuries to the keeper. Often these fish are most easily caught by lifting their favorite hiding place into a submerged pail or jar. If not, catch all species with a not too fine net and bring the net to the surface slowly. Do not lift the net from the water, but rather take a small container (such as a yogurt cup) and scoop the fish from the net. This keeps the stressed catfish from thrashing about and tangling its spines in the net.

If the fish is caught in the netting, first try leaving the net in a bucket without disturbing it. If this does not work, with many larger catfish, you could place the net onto a table, covered with a wet towel. Tightly grip the fish from the front with one hand and carefully unhook the net with your other hand. Catfish are tougher than most aquarium fish and will handle procedures such as this and being out of water well. Do not rush in order not to hurt yourself or the fish. Being out of water is less dangerous to the fish then an open wound or a ripped-out fin could be. If you are unable to untangle the fish, cut the net free with blunt-nosed children's scissors.

preferred foods are live insect larvae and worms, they will readily accept all foods offered to aquarium fish. To keep these shy

Auchenipterid habitat on the blackwater Rio Negro.

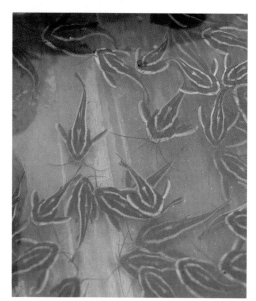

Striped raphaels at the tropical fish market in Iquitos, Peru.

nocturnal fish happy, they should be fed catfish tablets and sinking pellets after the lights go off.

Many species like to bury themselves in the gravel or sand substrate. While they do not eat plants, their active digging during the search for food can disturb plants. They show no aggression toward members of their own species.

Little or nothing is known about the reproduction of these catfish in captivity. At least some of the species are known to build bubble nests in the wild and practice some form of brood care. Sexing fish of this group is difficult, but adult females are heavier set and more rounded than the males. Several species are bred commercially in eastern Europe with the help of hormone injections. Although they come from soft and slightly acidic waters, they require no special water conditions.

Auchenipterichthys thoracatus, *the Zamora cat.*

The popular striped raphael, **Platydoras costatus.**

Helogenes marmoratus, *the wood catfish.*

Amaralia hypsiura, *the tadpole banjo cat.*

Centromochlus perugiae *is a striking community catfish.*

Whiptail banjo cat, **Platyastacus cotylephorus.**

= T I P =

Viewing Nocturnal Species

The fascinating behavior of nocturnal catfish is on display only once the tank lights are off. Setting up special dimmed lighting can offer a great opportunity to see the aquarium behavior of shy, nocturnal fish. Some experimentation may be necessary, depending on where your tank is and how it is set up. To start, try a dim light source near the tank to view your fish after the main lights are off. If your nocturnal fish do not find your room dark enough, using black lights or the type of red lights used in photography are a more involved but potentially rewarding option.

Platydoras costatus— the Striped Raphael

(Linnaeus 1758)

Widespread in the Amazon and Orinoco Basins

To 8 inches (20 cm)

Despite its relatively large size, the striped raphael is a good community fish that may be kept with larger tetras and barbs as well as cichlids of any kind.

Agamyxis pectinifrons— the Spotted Raphael

(Cope 1870)

Peru

To 6 inches (15 cm)

The spotted raphael is the most commonly encountered member of the group. Their maximum size makes them well suited to aquariums with fish larger than 1 inch (2.5 cm).

Amblydoras hancockii—the Talking Catfish, the Brown Raphael

(Valenciennes 1840)

Widespread from the Guyanas to Bolivia

Under 6 inches (15 cm)

The common or brown raphael is also a great community fish that is often available in stores. It is the smallest of the raphaels and is considered less shy than the other species.

Rhynchodoras xingui

(Klausewitz and Rössel 1961)

Rio Xingu, Brazil

Under 6 inches (15 cm)

This rare raphael is a striking addition to the aquarium. It is a somewhat bizarre looking, rarely seen catfish that is ideally adapted to eating small insect larvae from small crevices.

Auchenipteridae, the Naked Catfish

In nature, this group of catfish is rarely seen during the day unless their hiding places are disturbed. They spend the daylight hours wedged in hollow branches or in crevices of larger submerged wood. At night they can be seen actively swimming over the bottom or in the open water hunting for small prey.

In the aquarium, they are largely nocturnal but will come out to feed during the daylight hours. Overall they are less shy than raphael catfish. The fish from this group are most comfortable in small groups that patrol the aquarium at night. They will not harm plants and will eat any aquarium foods offered. Aquariums with naked cats must provide enough hiding places and caves in the form of driftwood, half coconut shells, and rock work for all animals to find hiding places.

Because naked catfish have neither scales nor bony plates, they have little protection against parasitic disease and are often among the first fish to fall ill if the aquarium population is affected by ich. All new additions to a tank containing naked cats should be well quarantined before their introduction to the community.

Like the *Doradiids,* they should be caught with a plastic container because the sharp dorsal and pectoral spines will get stuck in the net. The males may be recognized by more pronounced spines on the dorsal and pectoral fins. Several species of this group have been raised in captivity. Members of the group are egg layers with internal fertilization. Interestingly, the female lays the eggs a few weeks after they have been fertilized. The young hatch after several days and grow rapidly, feeding on the finest foods along the surface.

Auchenipterichthys thoracatus— the Zamora Catfish

(Kner 1858)
Amazon Basin
To 4 inches (10 cm)

This small species, very common in the wild, is the most frequently imported member of the group. While the fish is largely nocturnal, it will frequently be seen during the day in well-planted aquariums.

Entomocorus benjamini— Benjamin's Dwarf

(Eigenmann 1917)
Amazon, Peru, and Brazil
2 inches (5 cm)

Benjamin's dwarf is one of the smaller catfish for the community aquarium. Males have very long, thickened ventral fins.

Centromochlus perugiae— the Snowflake Catfish

(Steindachner 1882)
Peru
Maximum 2 inches (5 cm)

This striking little catfish has recently become popular among catfish enthusiasts, although it has yet to become readily available in the trade. Several successful spawnings of the species have occurred in well-planted species tanks of 10 to 15 gallons (35 to 55 L). It is only one of the many beautiful fish from this group.

Tatia aulopygia—the Naked Catfish

(Kner 1858)
Amazon Basin
3 inches (8 cm)

The common *Tatia* is much less attractive than others of the group. It is a hardy community fish that often gets overlooked because specimens hide at the dealers during the day.

Helogenidae, the Wood Catfish Group

Wood catfish are not popular in the aquarium trade, with only one occasional visitor to fish tanks.

Helogenes marmoratus— the Wood Catfish

(Günther 1863)
Widespread in the Amazon and Orinoco Basins, Guyanas
4 inches (10 cm)

This rarely imported catfish is hardy and easy to keep but almost impossible to observe during the daylight hours. Nevertheless, it is an interesting fish that will provide excellent if

Brachyrhamdia meesi *is found among schools of Corydoras.*

Bunocephalus coracoideus, *a secretive banjo cat.*

Microglanis *are rarely seen during the day.*

Bumble bee cat, Pseudopimelodus raninus.

discreet scavenging services in a community tank.

Aspredinidae, the Banjo Catfish

Banjo catfish are found across the Amazon Basin in areas of both low water flow and extreme shallows. Here they hunt for the smallest foods, such as worms and insect larvae. Since any fish on the move in shallow, still water has very little hope of avoiding predators (especially birds), banjo cats have evolved a strategy of remaining hidden, often by burying themselves in the fine sand. Water conditions in their natural habitats may vary. Generally, though, banjo catfish are found in water that is heavily stained by tannins and has an acidic pH and low hardness. Temperatures in the wild can vary greatly. Some species are found at cooler, higher elevations, while others inhabit the steamy Amazon lowlands. Many species in the group do not readily accept dry foods and must be started on and then slowly weaned off live tubifex worms or frozen mosquito larvae. These shy fish may

Hepapterus species are found in the leaf litter.

starve if kept in aquariums with too many other fish, as they compete poorly. *Bunocephalus coracoideus* has been bred in captivity, spawning in groups and producing large numbers of eggs that were not cared for by the adults. The young must be raised with the smallest foods.

Bunocephalus quadriradiatus— the Dwarf Banjo Catfish

(Mees 1989)
Rio Ucayali, Peru
Under 2 inches (5 cm)

This intriguing and tiny species is ideal for communities with even the smallest tetras and dwarf cichlids. They are rarely seen during the day unless fresh or frozen foods are fed.

Amaralia hypsiura— the Tadpole Banjo Catfish

(Kner 1855)
Amazon Basin
To 6 inches (15 cm)

There are dozens of species in the banjo catfish group, and many have never been exported for the aquarium hobby. *Amaralia* are

bizarre catfish that can rarely be seen moving unless food is offered at night. The fish can be picked up by hand even in the wild and will simply curl up and remain curled for some time when dropped back into the water.

Bunocephalus coracoideus— the Common Banjo Catfish

(Cope 1874)
Amazon Basin
To 6 inches (15 cm)

This is the most commonly imported and available representative of the group. On the

Dupuoichthys sapito, a small banjo cat.

occasions when it can be seen, it is a curiosity for any community aquarium with nonaggressive fish. Despite its larger size this banjo cat is not a threat to smaller aquarium inhabitants. Many an aquarist has purchased this odd and attractive catfish out of a bare, glass-bottomed aquarium store tank, only to have it disappear once it finds itself with sand to go under. The initial disappointment of having bought a vanishing fish can be replaced with surprise when the fish reappears weeks later, larger and much more active. Some individual specimens will go through a hiding phase when first brought home and then become, if not gregarious, at least visible for a short period every day.

Bunocephalus verrucosus— the Hunchback Banjo Catfish

(Bloch 1794)
Widespread in the Guyanas and Amazon Basin
To 4 inches (10 cm)

The smaller hunchback banjo cat is rarely intentionally exported but almost always comes in mixed in shipments of the common banjo cat. It is in that odd class of aquarium fish that sell well because sharp-eyed and curious hobbyists are quick to grab anything that appears different and unexpected when it is mixed in with better-known animals. The possibility that something interesting to keep, but not well-known, can be found in even the smallest, unspecialized pet stores is one of the key attractions of catfish keeping.

Platystacus cotylephorus— the Whiptail Banjo

(Bloch 1794)
Coastal rivers of northern Brazil
To 10 inches (25 cm)

Perhaps the most easily recognizable member of the group is the whiptail banjo catfish. Including the extremely long thin tail, the fish will grow to 10 inches (25 cm) in length. It is found in coastal zones and will tolerate brackish (mixed fresh and salt) water. The whiptail banjo is not a threat to other aquarium fish, even if they are much smaller.

Pimelodidae—Pimelodus and Others

Pimelodus are active swimmers found in almost every pet store. Specimens must be examined closely before purchase, as they are scaleless fish that are easily infested with ich. The fine barbels may also be injured by sharp gravel, which can lead to bacterial infections.

Well-chosen specimens are among the easiest catfish to feed in the aquarium. They readily eat any food offered.

A word of warning—the spines on the dorsal and pectoral fins are very sharp and may cause injuries if the fish are not handled carefully. A protein in the fish may cause allergic reactions in some people, so the fish must be handled very carefully. They should be caught with a plastic container or scooped into a submerged container from the net so they do not entangle themselves hopelessly.

None of the easy to capture small pimelodids are reproduced commercially for the hobby. The group contains some of the biggest fish in South America. Both the red-tail cat *(Phractocephalus hemioliopterus)* and tiger shovelnose *(Pseudoplatystoma spp.)* from this group are important food fish, commercially produced on fish farms by the use of hormone injections. Unfortunately, specimens of these big cats do sometimes find their way into the aquarium trade. The more reasonably sized species are extremely popular.

Pimelodus pictus—the Spotted Pim

(Steindachner 1876)
Amazon and Orinoco Basins
To 6 inches (15 cm) in captivity

This fish is one of the most widely available aquarium catfish, although it is really a far from ideal aquarium resident. The popular pictus cats are voracious predators that will eat tetras and can bother other aquarium inhabitants at night with their long barbels. They are hardy fish for aquariums with larger fish such as midsized cichlids, larger characins, and other tough fish. Pimelodus are also active during the day. In the aquarium, the fish will stay at less than 6 inches (15 cm) in total length, but they get larger in nature.

Pseudopimelodus raninus— the Bumblebee Catfish

(Valenciennes 1840)
Amazon Basin and Guyanas
To 4 inches (10 cm)

In spite of it being a shy, nocturnal species, the bumblebee cat will prey on small fish. Adults are not big, but they are resourceful when hungry. They are best kept in small groups.

Microglanis iheringi— the Dwarf Bumblebee Catfish

(Gomes 1946)
Orinoco River Basin
2.5 inches (6 cm)

The dwarf bumblebee cat is a good aquarium resident that may frequently be seen during

TIP

Exotic-Needs Catfish

Owners should know where their fish are from, as that simplifies the planning of the tank. Any well-informed dealer will have easy access to information on an exotic cat's point of origin. Most *Loricariids* are adaptable to good general aquarium conditions, but there are some fish with specific needs. Most suckermouths from the Xingu, Tocantins, and Tapajos Rivers are more comfortable in tanks with a current so strong that finding fish to keep them company can be extremely challenging. Compromising on water flow for these species is possible if the aquarist remembers that strongly flowing water is rich in oxygen. By adding extra air stones, doing very frequent water changes, and adding one or two power heads in a larger tank to provide a directional flow, a community can be built around these lovely cats. A general principle of aquarium keeping is to prioritize the needs of the most demanding fish in the tank and choose tank mates that can adapt to the conditions this species demands. If you choose to keep Xingu, Tocantins, or Tapajos suckermouths, they will be the centerpiece fish in your setup.

the day, when food is offered. This opportunistic species will consider fry and tiny aquarium fish as prey. Its nocturnal hunting strategy is deadly for fish like cichlids, which must be able to see fry predators if they are to protect their young.

The Amazon in rainy season.

*Some **Plecostomus** can get a touch bigger than we might expect.*

*One of the dreaded **Candiru** cats,* **Tridensimilis nemurus.**

Brochis splendens, *a larger cory-like cat.*

Corydoras paleatus, *the salt and pepper cory, is a long-time favorite.*

Corydoras arcuatus *is the strikingly marked "skunk" cory.*

Brachyrhamdia meesi—the Imitator Catfish

(Sands and Black 1985)
Peru and Western Brazil
To 3 inches (8 cm)

One of the more interesting catfish, in evolutionary terms, imitators occur together with *Corydoras* in nature. There are several species of *Brachyrhamdia* that mimic different species of *Corydoras*. Predictably, these hard-to-find cats are best kept in small groups with the *Corydoras* species they resemble.

Loricariids, the Suckermouth Catfishes

In the early days of the aquarium hobby, there was a popular catfish called the "pleco." It was kept as an algae eater, although observant aquarists noted the fish from one store would eat algae while those from another might not. They also seemed to grow to different sizes. It was not long before these supposed "algae eaters" started to attract not only fans but attention. Exploration of the rivers of Amazonia began to turn up a delightful variety of separate and distinctive species. This happened so quickly the aquarium hobby was scarcely able to keep up.

Unfortunately, the myth of the single species "pleco" seems to persist in many pet shops where the not very helpful popular name lives on. In spite of everything hobbyists are learning about this group, some pet shops and dealers still sell the babies of large species like *Pterogoplichthys* and *Hypostomus* to unsuspecting tank owners who then face the impossible task of finding a place for a foot-long (30 cm) monster one year later. A little knowledge can help you find a little catfish.

While local pet shop "plecos" are inappropriately lumped together and sold as cheap bread-and-butter fish, specialist dealers ask for and get astronomical prices for the beautiful *Loricariid* catfish coming out of South America now. The information gap between the expert hobbyist and the beginner is very wide in the world of these catfish, although many of the currently uncommon species are easy enough to keep. No matter how many labels we make for them, these fish will always defy easy description. Along with *Corydoras,* the suckermouth catfishes are showing us a bewildering richness in newly discovered species, varieties, mysteries, and possibilities. No other group of catfish has as much variety in shape and color.

The authors hope this manual can serve as a bridge, to introduce some of these wonderful fish while stimulating hobbyists to seek out the many rich sources of *Loricariid* information on the Internet, in print, and in the knowledge of catfish fanciers in local aquarium clubs.

Additional Catfish Species

In the following section are many species that remain small and make excellent aquarium fish. Not all of them are useful algae eaters for the aquarium. One only has to consider the bulk of a 3-inch (8-cm) *Loricariid* and then consider how much algae the average home aquarium can reasonably generate for them. Fish keepers must keep in mind that many "plecos" are omnivores that need to be fed directly and will not survive on algae and leftovers from the other fish.

For *Loricariids,* the decor of their tanks is as important as it is for the more famous cichlids. Many need caves to build their territories

TIP

Sexing Some Common Catfish

Identifying the sex of a lot of catfish is not easy. With the more common types, there are some loose guidelines. Most healthy *Corydoras* are easily sexed from the top. In general, males have sharper features—when viewing specimens from the top, think of a speedboat. Females are more rounded and wide around the flanks. From the top, think of the general outline of a tugboat. In some cory species, nature has cooperated in other ways. Sometimes males will have longer and more pronounced fins as well.

Male *Loricariids* have wider heads and thicker pectoral spines. Often there are a greater number of odontodes (spines) on the pectorals and on the side of the head. These spines can look like sideburns. In some groups such as *Ancistrus,* males develop long tentacles on the head.

Then again, in other, less common and therefore less studied species and groups, even the experts do not have a clear system for telling the sexes apart.

digestive processes, in much the same way as birds need gravel. As would be expected for large algae eaters, they can have a general taste for vegetable matter. Some of them will eat or damage plants, and many will eat algae only when they are juveniles or starving.

Anyone wishing to keep "plecos" properly must find supplementary foods that allow the often shy and slower "plecos" to eat without the other fish eating their food first. The easiest way is to feed with the lights off, when most fish in the aquarium are asleep. Commercially prepared, specialized foods (usually in wafer or stick form) that are preferred by suckermouths are available. These will entice even the most timid fish to come out during the day.

When it comes to size, suckermouth catfish are a very varied group, ranging from just 1 inch (2.5 cm) (*Parotocinclus* spp. from Peru) to over 4 feet (120 cm) (*Acanthicus hystrix)*. We have concentrated on smaller species that either are, or should be popular and that all make excellent aquarium fish. They have been divided into three subgroups. First, we have the "true plecos." These have the traditional shape aquarists expect from pet shop "plecos." Second, there is a loose group of species that live on sandy stream, lake, and river bottoms or on plants. Finally, we will have a look at the increasingly popular and appreciated dwarf algae eaters around the genus *Otocinclus*.

around. Others need driftwood. It was long believed that these catfish actually ate wood fibers as an essential food. This is now being questioned. However, it does seem clear that they prosper when they can at the very least feed off the surface organisms that colonize submerged wood. For many species, the roughage provided by wood is a part of their

Peckoltia, Ancistrus, and Others

This group is the cutting edge when it comes to new catfish discoveries. There have been so many species found in recent years that scientists have been unable to keep up with the

Parotocinclus *sp. "Pernambuco" is a superb algae-eater.*

The pitbull **Plecostomus** *does not have a scientific name.*

Parotocinclus eppleyi.

Rineloricaria *are easy beginner catfish.*

Farlowella are commonly kept, but often mistreated due to misinformation.

Otocinclus vestitus, *an algae eater from the floating meadows of the South American rainforest.*

Sturisoma festivum, *the elegant royal farlowella.*

Acistridium, *the rare green stick catfish.*

classification of newcomers. Many of these fish have no internationally accepted, standard name. For a number of years now, a German aquarium magazine *(DATZ)* has been publishing photos of the new *Loricariids* and assigning each one a number until the fish can be described. In the short term, this at least allows us to identify species while we wait for scientists to get to the classification of these curious and diverse animals. Once a fish has been studied and officially named, the number is no longer needed to describe the fish. The number is then basically retired. However, the process is very slow moving.

We have chosen to include these "L" numbers in order to help the reader search for more information on the fish. Often people will simply refer to the "L" number of a fish instead of its trade or even scientific name. In a way, the "L" numbers have become the popular names of these creatures. For those who might be inclined to see this system as pretentious or, more cynically, as a pet trade marketing device, *Loricariids* are not just differentiated by colors or external characteristics. This is a scientifically based system, albeit a temporary one. The mouth shape is a key piece of information. The many slight variations in the structure are used not only to feed but also to hold on in extreme currents. It is worth pointing out that at the time of this writing, more than 350 fish have received "L" numbers!

Peckoltia vittata—the Clown Pleco
(Steindachner 1881)
Peru and Colombia
5 inches (13 cm)

The clown pleco has been readily available to hobbyists for a long time and should not be an expensive choice. They are shy aquarium residents that take a long time to get used to their surroundings. Their small size and extremely peaceful behavior makes them perfect fish for the community aquarium. Clown plecos have occasionally bred in captivity in the typical fashion for the group, with the male guarding the eggs after a spawning in a cave. On a positive note, they will not damage most plants. However, the downside is they are only moderate algae eaters, with a taste for generally high-quality tropical fish foods in the aquarium and for small insects in the wild.

Zonancistrus pulcher— Butterfly Pleco, L 52
(Steindachner 1915)
Rio Negro, Rio Atabapo, Rio Cassiquare.
6 inches (13 cm)

This was one of the first fancy plecos to be exported, helping to open the door for the flood that was to follow. It stands out in the group because it is found in mineral-poor blackwater rivers with very acidic pH. In this water chemistry, no plants survive and only little algae grows on rocks. The butterfly pleco's flat body shape allows it to spend the day hidden in crevices. It comes out at night to feed. Butterfly plecos are perfect aquarium inhabitants for tanks with acidic water species like *Apistogramma* dwarf cichlids or *Discus*. They are shy but good community tank fish that will eat some algae. In breeding season, male *zonancistrus* develop pronounced spines (odontodes) on their pectoral fins. Females have wider, shorter bodies. While they may be easy to sex, to date there have been no reports of this attractive species being bred in the aquarium.

Hypancistrus zebra—Zebra Pleco, L 46
(Isbrücker and Nijssen 1991)
Rio Xingu, Brazil.
3 inches (8 cm)

This is perhaps the most sought-after species of all suckermouths. When the fish were first discovered in the late eighties, they caused a huge sensation that started the pleco craze. They were the "cover fish" of almost every aquarium magazine, as their sharply defined color pattern rivals the beauty of coral reef fish. The possibility there could be other undiscovered gems like the zebra pleco drew the attention of fish collectors directly to catfish. This was a rewarding new direction for the commercial industry, as the Rio Xingu has turned out to be a treasure chest of catfishes with dozens of spectacular L-species exported in recent years.

Despite their diminutive size (especially when they are imported), the zebra pleco is a territorial fish that requires very good water quality and special care. *Hypancistrus* do not need algae. They do have quick metabolisms and need to be fed frequently or they will waste away. They are not garbage cleaners for crowded community tanks and would best be placed into a tank where they can be the dominant species. Such a tank should be set up with plenty of hiding places and as much current as possible. Zebra plecos are not shy fish and will come out frequently during the day.

Wild stocks of the species may be in trouble from pollution, deforestation, and overfishing. The habitat seems relatively restricted, and popularity has been a problem for this fish. While it dropped from being one of the most expensive aquarium fish to a more reasonable level in recent years, prices are on the way up again. Aquarium breeding of this beauty may be the only way we will have access to specimens in the future.

In nature, zebras live in fast flowing water together with *Ancistrus ranunculus,* the weird, wonderful, and larger Medusa pleco. Divers catch these fancy plecos one by one, in the clear deep water of the Rio Xingu.

Parancistrus aurantiacus— the Black Rubber Pleco
(Castelnau 1855)
Eastern Brazil
7 inches (18 cm)

As the popular name implies, the black rubber pleco is not going to turn heads among any but the greatest *Loricariid* fans. While it is among the least colorful of the commonly found plecos, it is an excellent and hardy community fish. The strong armor plates over their backs and flanks, as well as their short fins, make the fish ideal for the company of aggressive cichlids and characins. Juveniles are excellent algae eaters, but adults tend to have less interest in cleaning up, looking instead for more robust foods. The species has not yet reproduced in captivity. There is a bright orange form of this fish found in the Rio Xingu that is exported on rare occasions. However, the highly priced fish lose their attractive coloration in the aquarium and quickly fade to the uniform black color of the common form.

Chaetostoma thomsoni— the Green Rubber Pleco
(Regan 1904)
Rio Magdalena, Colombia
3 inches (8 cm)

Members of the genus *Chaetostoma* are widespread in South America. Some species are

Otocinclus *sp. "zebra" is an uncommon beauty.*

Hypoptopoma *species from the Rio Huallaga.*

found in the Peruvian Andes, as high up as 6,500 feet (2,000 m) above sea level, in water temperatures of less than 59°F (15°C). *Chaetostoma* are hardy aquarium fish that make excellent algae eaters. They will not harm hardy plants. They are especially fond of vegetables, such as fresh lettuce leaves and potato slices. *Chaetostoma* prefer aquarium temperatures of less than 75°F (23.8°C). They have spawned in the aquarium on rare occasions, with the male guarding the small clutch of eggs laid on the roof of a rock cave in a strong current.

Ancistrus dolichopterus— the Bristlenose Pleco
(Kner 1854)
Eastern Amazonia
5 inches (13 cm)

Ancistrus are the ideal aquarium suckermouths. The only problem is identifying them. *Ancistrus dolichopterus* is one of those species with a long pedigree in the aquarium hobby. They often appeared, with blurry photos, in older aquarium literature as one of the two or three aquarium trade *Ancistrus* known at the time.

Aquarists and dealers tended to refer to those pictures, see what their new fish resembled most, and slap a convenient and familiar name on them. Most small *Ancistrus* species have been sold as *dolichopterus* at one time or another.

The real *A. dolichopterus* is small. They will not harm most tough-leafed aquarium plants and make excellent algae eaters. In addition, they are hardy fish that adapt to almost any water conditions. Males defend small territories against their own species and, in the aquarium, are very partial to flowerpots. The fish are best kept in small groups of 3 or 4 fish per 40 gallons (150 L). Many breeders use juvenile ancistrus to clean up tanks with young fry of other fish.

No other pleco has been bred as frequently as the bristlenose. It is one of few catfish bred commercially, mostly in Europe, although there is a cottage industry in *Ancistrus* production by catfish enthusiasts worldwide. They are easy to coax into spawning. Watching the male guard his bright orange wrigglers is a delightful sight. As a result of their easy reproduction in captivity, there are breeder selected varieties in gold and marbled patterns as well as albino and long-finned sorts available. If breeding this

Hypoptopoma gulare.

The gold Ancistrus *is a popular catfish.*

fish interests you (and it should), please see the special description in the breeding chapter.

Ancistrus ranunculus—the Medusa Pleco, L 34

(Muller, Rapp Py-Daniel, and Zuanon, 1994)
Rio Xingu, Brazil
6 inches (15 cm)

The bizarre looking but weirdly beautiful Medusa pleco is found in the deep flowing water of the Rio Xingu. Here they are superbly adapted for thin crevices between rocks and high currents. Males develop huge heads covered in soft tentacles. In many ways, for those who like the bristles on bristlenoses, this fish surpasses all expectations. L 34 is a good algae eater and can be kept with hardy characins and most cichlids. To date, the species has been bred only on rare occasions. This makes it a little hard to get, but it is well worth any trouble.

Ancistrus claro—the Gold Marble Pleco, LDA 08

(Knaack 1999)
Rio Cuiaba, Brazil
2.5 inches (6 cm)

This beautiful little *Ancistrus* is not available as often as its attractiveness calls for. Hopefully, that will change soon. Gold marbles are one of the smallest members of the genus and also one of the most attractively colored. They are ideal algae eaters for the planted community aquarium or for tanks with small cichlids. The gold marble *Ancistrus* has been bred on several occasions, but aquarists are still dependent on wild importations to get this fish.

Ancistrus claro, *LDA 08.*

Ancistrus hoplogenys—the White Seam Bristlenose Pleco

(Günther 1864)
Rio Negro, Brazil
5 inches (13 cm)

The white seam *Ancistrus* is a striking species from blackwater habitats. The young have bright white spots and wide seams along the edges of the caudal and dorsal fins, making them especially striking plecos for the community aquarium. White seams are good algae eaters that are very active during the day. Unfortunately, they are less frequently bred than the common *Ancistrus*.

Lithoxancistrus tigris—L 275

(Armbruster and Provenzano 2000)
Rio Orinoco
6 inches (15 cm)

The search for new catfish never seems to stop and constantly produces impressive results. This species is a recent discovery in the Rio Orinoco, where a group of colorful suckermouths has evolved in a situation similar to that of Brazil's Xingu and Tapajos Rivers. This flat-bodied *Loricariid* is adapted for life in narrow crevices among the boulders on the Rio Orinoco. As this is being written, the fish is an expensive rarity from a region where fish exports are uncommon. It is clear that we have not seen anywhere near all the catfishes that are quietly living their lives in the waters of South America.

Baryancistrus spp.—the Gold Nugget Plecos, L 18, L 81, and L 177

Undescribed
Rio Xingu, Rio Iriri Brazil
7 inches (18 cm)

This group of plecos is widespread in the Rio Xingu, Rio Iriri, and Rio Tapajos in Brazil, where they are caught in great numbers in rapids. They are hardy aquarium residents with a great appetite for algae, cucumbers, freshly cut potatoes, and other vegetables. To date, they have been rarely bred in the aquarium.

Loricaridae spp.—the Blue and Green Plecos, L 128 and L 200

Undescribed.
Rio Orinoco
7 inches (18 cm)

The blue pleco is found north on the Rio Orinoco in the Raudales Artures rapids near Puerto Ayacucho, near the border between Colombia and Venezuela. Farther south, a second form of perhaps the same species is found, but their coloration is greener. Both are excellent algae eaters that thrive in strong currents.

Sturisoma, Loricaria, and Others

The slender, elegant shape of these fish make them curious aquarium residents. They are very often imported as strange looking catfish will always find a receptive market. They are peaceful and extremely tolerant toward plants, despite their size. These elegant catfish enjoy feedings of lettuce or fresh peas. They will also eat flake foods, sinking pellets, and frozen foods.

Sturisoma festivum— the Royal Farlowella

(Myers 1942)
Colombia
To 8 inches (20 cm)

The royal farlowella is one of the most stately looking of all catfish. Aquariums for *Sturisoma* should have some vertical basking spaces in the form of rocks or driftwood. A look at their shape and coloration will tell you a lot about their environmental needs. What many do not realize is that aquariums that are too densely planted or decorated are not ideal because the awkwardly swimming *Sturisoma* will have trouble moving around. The fish may be the picture of dignity when still, but when they decide to travel in open water, they will never be mistaken for a ballet dancer. Mature males develop interesting sideburns of fine bristles on the sides of their heads. The royal farlowella breeds frequently and easily, depositing bright green eggs onto vertical surfaces or even onto the glass. See the breeding section for a detailed description about this fish.

Hemiloricaria morrowi— Loricaria

(Fowler 1940)
Rio Ucayali, Peru
5 inches (13 cm)

This commonly imported fish is ideal for community tanks with small fish. They are busy around the clock and pick up leftover foods. In effect, this is a catfish that does scavenge. They are often reasonably priced fish that do not stand out in bare, overly bright pet shop tanks. Once at home in less stressed surroundings, they usually turn into active favorites in the tank. Many species of the genus *Hemiloricaria* are exported, and identification is not always easy. The group is not too difficult to breed and will spawn in narrow tubes of 1-inch (2.5 cm) diameter where the male guards both the eggs and the young.

Lamontichthys filamentosus— the Threadfin Farlowella

(La Monte 1935)
Amazon Basin
8 inches (20 cm)

All members of the group have some filaments on the tips of their fins, but this species is the most spectacular found so far. All fins have long extensions that give the threadfin an extremely elegant look. The exact purpose of these extensions is not known, but they may help with orientation in the murky water. *Lamontichthys* need high flow and lots of oxygen. They may be kept with other peaceful species that need similar conditions. To date, nothing is known about their breeding habits.

Hemiodontichthys acipenserinus— the Pinocchio Farlowella

(Kner 1854)
Peruvian Amazon
7 inches (18 cm)

This odd looking fish will burrow into the substrate and spend the whole day sifting through fine sand looking for small particles of food. The species rarely leaves the bottom. It is one of many interesting *Loricariid* types exported from Peru, recently bred in the aquarium for the first time.

Farlowella amazona— the Twig Catfish

(Günther 1864)
Amazonia
8 inches (20 cm)

In any flowing river, floating branches and long twigs will collect as they snag on fallen trees or collect in swirling eddies. A fish that mimics a twig will obviously find a great home

Corydoras fowleri *is a beautiful long-snouted cory.*

Ancistrus ranunculus, L34, the Medusa catfish, is a prehistoric-looking beast.

Peckoltia sp. L204 from Peru.

in such habitats. Hobbyists often miss clues like body shape when they look at fish in bare aquarium shop tanks. The twig catfish is often misunderstood by aquarium enthusiasts. Despite its seemingly inactive lifestyle, the species needs high flow and lots of oxygen. If these conditions are met, twig catfish spring to life, actively rasping algae on all surfaces of the aquarium. Imported specimens may be from several species in the group. They do not do well in crowded community tanks, which leads to their having an undeserved reputation as difficult aquarium fish.

Otocinclus and Others

These *Otocinclus* are generally available, inexpensive, and useful fish. These tiny dynamos are magnificent algae eaters for tanks with companion fish not large enough to try to eat them. In a way, they are victims of their own usefulness. The common oto is a fairly drab fish that is kept for a function. The recent arrival of a number of attractive newly discovered species has generally been met with a large yawn. Aquarists do not expect their otos to be beautiful and seemingly will not make the effort to track down the new beauties. As this is being written, most of the new oto species are rarely kept specialists' fish, renowned among those in the know, but rarely explored by the average hobbyist.

Otocinclus vestitus—
Otto Cat, Oto Cat, Oto

(Regan 1904)
Amazon Basin
1.5 inches (3.8 cm)

These *Otocinclus* are great little fish that are regularly caught by the thousands in floating meadows and in rest waters of the Amazon.

These hardy aquarium cleaners are among the best choices to fight unwanted algae. Their small mouths do not harm aquarium plants, and the perky little fish are active all day. As a general formula for a planted tank with small inhabitants, one *Otocinclus* should be kept per 5 gallons (20 L) of water, bearing in mind that these sociable little fish are most comfortable in a troop of at least six. *Otocinclus* species are difficult to tell apart, and many species are imported under the one name. Despite their popularity, they have not often been bred in the aquarium. They tend to be taken for granted, as are most inexpensive species. Spawning and raising otos would be a coup for the ambitious fish breeder.

Parotocinclus sp. "Pernambuco"

Undescribed
Pernambuco, Brazil
2 inches (5 cm)

This hardy fish will unfortunately damage soft-leafed plants but makes an otherwise good algae eater. They can also be used in aquariums with more alkaline water than other *Otocinclus.*

Parotocinclus eppleyi—
the Starlight Oto

(Schaefer and Provenzano 1993)
Rio Orinoco
1.5 inches (3.8 cm)

The starlight *Parotocinclus* is more than just a fish with a lovely, popular name. It is an ultimate fast-water fish. In nature, they live in shallow and extremely clear water on sunken logs and roots where the current is strongest. Their heads are sloped, which, in combination with a current, works to push the fish down against the substrate as it feeds on algae. As would be expected, in the aquarium, they need plenty of oxygen and lots of water flow. In tanks that are not set up this way, the fish often die off "mysteriously." Of interest is that some farlowella are found in the same algae-rich wild habitat.

Hypoptopoma gulare— the Giant Otocinclus
(Cope 1878)
Peru, Colombia, and Venezuela
3 inches (8 cm)

The giant Otocinclus is only an oto in its popular name, as scientifically, it is in another genus altogether. The tendency for some scientific names to sometimes take on a life of their own is at its worst with names like "plecostomus" (which no longer exists as a valid name) but occurs with fish like this as well. The giant oto is an interesting aquarium fish that is not exported often. They are found in reed beds and floating meadows and adapt well to community tanks with hardy plants. Their larger size makes them good candidates for algae control in tanks with fish that would harass parotocinclus, but in spite of this, they still have not caught on. This is a shame, as the commercial aquarium trade still brings in fish like the Asian barb-relative Gyrinocheilus aymonieri, the Chinese algae eater, an aggressive ugly species that does not even consistently eat algae. To date, giant otos have only sporadically been bred in captivity.

Corydoras and Armored Catfish

When it comes to hobbyists who specialize in cats, there are two main groups—those who like suckermouth cats and the fans of "corys" and their close relatives. While we may admire the ornate patterning or weird shapes of other catfish, there is something hard to define in the appeal of the small armored catfish of the group Callichthyidae. What draws us into keeping them is very often their shapes. Most corys are squat creatures with the same instant attractiveness as a number of small, round mammals. Add their attractive "faces," their moustache-like barbels, and their most unfish-like eyes (which rotate in their sockets, giving us an apparent cory wink), and a strictly scientific approach to observing and learning about nature through the aquarium can fly out the window.

These animals draw one into anthropomorphism—projecting human characteristics onto animals. Discussing them without using words like "personality" can be very difficult.

The science of armored cats is waiting once we begin to dig. These little fish are an amazing evolutionary success story. They are widespread throughout northern South America and have produced more species and varieties than we are currently able to catalogue. To begin a serious study of Corydoras, Aspidoras, and Brochis is to open a vast world of infinite detail and variety.

Even newcomers to the hobby can profit from this diversity, as rare and undescribed species turn up in even the smallest pet stores. Wild cory species school together, get caught together, and are sold together. There is also a lively specialist trade in the high-end rarities, both through importers and hobbyist breeders.

Armored cats feature some interesting anatomical adaptations. Their body armor is strong enough that decomposed specimens will

Peckoltia vittata *is among the most common small* **Plecostomus.**

Aspidoras *need oxygenated waters, and are great jumpers.*

Chaetostoma *species are good algae eaters.*

Hypancistrus *sp. "L260, Queen Arabesque" is an ornate and exotic beauty.*

Aspidoras, *the rarely imported cousin of the corys.*

sometimes leave behind hard, rigid, ghostlike shapes. They have sharp defensive spines in their pectoral and dorsal fins, which they spread when they perceive danger. They can be tough on hands and nets as well as on the mouths and throats of predators. They can, and must, breathe surface air, extracting oxygen through their intestines as they literally swallow air, often several times per minute. While thousands of aquarists have successfully spawned and raised corys, no one is 100 percent certain of how they fertilize their eggs. Theories abound, but it remains one of the unsolved mysteries of the aquarium world.

A manual of this size can only show some representative species, but hopefully, will serve to launch at least a few of its readers into this great corner of the catfish hobby. Like most hobbyists, we will start with an old favorite, the ever available:

Corydoras aeneus—the Bronze Cory
(Gill 1858)
Northern South America and Trinidad
2.5 inches (6 cm)

Corydoras aeneus is a tough little animal, known to survive for many years in aquariums that do not get the care and attention they deserve. More delicate tank mates may come and go, but an *aeneus* will often carry on. Its basic colors are a nondescript gray and green (although an albino form is as popular as the original animal). Yet it is one of the most popular aquarium fish in the trade. Its charms lie in how easy it is to breed (and therefore mass produce cheaply), its hardiness, and its active behavior. Most aquarium shops regularly carry this long-popular catfish.

Since it is a wide ranging species, it has proven to do what *Corydoras* do best—vary. There are hard to find but very attractive *aeneus* type corys appearing in the trade now. They may someday be classed as new species. These include a form with a neon green stripe, a fish with bright orange flashes on the side of its head, an orange striped fish, and a black *aeneus*. A recent rediscovery sold as the red stripe *aeneus* has now been identified as *Corydoras venezuelanus* (Ihering 1911).

The standard *aeneus* forms are excellent scavengers in a community, though like all *Corydoras,* they can never be considered as garbage cleaners. These fish feed on food that makes it to the substrate. It is their keeper's responsibility to see that enough good food makes it to these bottom dwellers. Like most cory species, they are best kept in groups of six. Solitary specimens can live almost unnoticed for years, but a group of these sociable animals provides a constant, dynamic, and apparently quite happy show.

Corydoras arcuatus—the Skunk Cory
(Elwin 1939)
Upper Amazon River Basin
2 inches (5 cm)

Corydoras arcuatus is a more delicate species that is gaining in popularity due to its striking color pattern. Their sandy-colored bodies are topped with an arching black stripe from the nose to the tail. This accentuates the computer mouse shape of the fish (already a selling point in corys). However, given the difficulty in breeding this touchy species, seasonally available specimens in pet shops are usually much more expensive than their more adaptable relatives.

This cory can serve as an introduction to an intriguing sideshow in the *Corydoras* world. It seems that for a great number of *Corydoras* species, there are long- and short-snouted versions, sharing similar color patterns and habitats but differing in size and behavior. Many long- or sharp-snouted species get considerably bigger than their regular neighbors. They can also be quite territorial, standing the stereotype of the cute, gentle little *Corydoras* on its head. However, they are also very fine looking fish. *Corydoras arcuatus* has an attractive, undescribed, long-nosed form and is also very similar to the robust (and currently quite rare and expensive) *Corydoras narcissus* (Nijissen and Isbrücker 1980).

Corydoras julii
Corydoras melanistius
Corydoras trilineatus—
the Spotted Corydoras
(Steindachner 1906), (Regan 1912), and (Cope 1872)
Throughout Amazonia
2 to 3 inches (5 to 8 cm)

What is in a name? Not much when it comes to the aquarium trade and *Corydoras* with spots. Like many fish from Guiana, *Corydoras melanistius* had its aquarium glory days before the Brazilian fish-exporting industry became established. *Corydoras julii* was a name applied to almost any Brazilian spotted cory in the North American fish trade in the early days of Amazon exports and, as such, is one of the few species with a consistent presence in older aquarium manuals. *Corydoras trilineatus* seems to have picked up the slack as the king of the misidentified pet shop fish since those days. In effect, if it is a cory and has spots, many a

dealer will sell it as one of these three and not worry about key identification clues like point of origin, spot patterning, placement of black blotches, or size.

Since most spotted corys have similar needs, this is not a big problem for the hobbyist. If one keeps groups of these little fish in clean water with some hiding places and offers them nutritious food, their endless bustle will add a lot to your enjoyment of the aquarium. This misidentification can be an advantage to sharp-eyed aquarists who like to do research and collect oddities. The catfish keepers' edition of a good fishing trip can be a trip to a shop with several poorly tagged and therefore inexpensive *Corydoras* species. Identifying them after the fact can be entertaining, especially as playing this game with the often equally misidentified cichlids can backfire and lead to your purchasing an eventual behemoth that will demolish your tank. Cory keeping never leads to such disturbing surprises. This group of cory cats will always fit into a community and will only surprise you with the details of their attractive markings.

Corydoras paleatus—
the Salt–and–Pepper Cory,
the Peppered Corydoras
(Jenyns 1842)
Uruguay, Argentina, and Southern Brazil
2 inches (5 cm)

As you head south from Amazonia, the climate becomes more temperate. *Corydoras paleatus* is a representative of the subtropical corys, as it does well in an unheated home aquarium. Indeed, they do not necessarily adapt well to the warmer ranges of the heated home aquarium. In a room temperature tank,

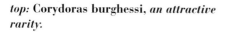

top: **Corydoras burghessi,** *an attractive rarity.*

above: **Corydoras aeneus** *is one of several corys with commercially produced albino forms.*

middle right: **Corydoras panda** *is a small member of the family.*

bottom right: **Corydoras reticulatus.**

top: **Corydoras aeneus** *is THE cory of the hobby.*

middle: **Corydoras pygmaeus** *has some surprising habits for a Cory.*

bottom: **Dianema urostriata,** *an uncommon aquarium inhabitant.*

they are very tough little creatures. This, as well as the ease with which they can be farmed, has made them the main rival of *Corydoras aeneus* in the inexpensive catfish trade. While not the most striking cory, they are one of the easiest both to find and to keep.

Corydoras panda—the Panda Cory
(Nijssen and Isbrücker 1971)
Rio Ucayali, Peru
Under 2 inches (5 cm)

Yesterday's expensive rarity has become a staple fish of the aquarium, largely because this beautiful little animal is not difficult to breed. Pandas are the smallest of the corys encountered so far in this manual and can be considered the most commonly available representative of a number of small *Corydoras*. They are not as small as the true pygmy *Corydoras* group, which in effect improves their position as commonly kept fish. When maintained in schools, these active little cats are a wonderful addition to any community of small and gentle fishes.

Corydoras robustus
(Nijssen and Isbrücker 1980)
Purus River Basin (Mid-Amazonia)
3 inches (8 cm)

Although *C. panda* is a small cory, *C. robustus* opens another door, this time for a peek at the larger species. The large cory cats are rarely kept and can be extremely hard to locate in pet shops. Some, like the attractive but heat intolerant *C. barbatus* (a mountain stream fish that needs water cooler than 70°F [20°C]), are extremely difficult to ship. Others just do not fit the profile of an aquarium cory and are overlooked by exporters and importers alike.

Large corys are specialist fish for those with experience keeping the group.

Corydoras sterbai—the Gold-fin Cory, the Orange-fin Cory
(Knaack 1962)
Central Brazil and Bolivia
2.5 inches (6 cm)

This cory is a high-bodied chunk of beautifully colored armored catfish. Luckily, prices for this fairly recent import are falling fast, as they are proving easy to breed, at least for those prepared to allow the slow-growing animals to reach maturity. Tank-bred specimens are rapidly supplanting wild imports in the aquarium trade. *C. sterbai* does very well in a tank with smaller community fish and is kept very much like *C. aeneus*. Given its bulky, high-bodied form, *C. sterbai* should not be overly crowded. This is no problem, as half a dozen of these active and pretty corys can function as the centerpiece species of any aquarium setup.

Corydoras pygmaeus
Corydoras hastatus
Corydoras habrosus
the Pygmy Corys, the Tetra Corys
(Knaack 1966), (Eigenmann and Eigenmann 1888), and (Weitzman 1960)
Amazonia
Under 1 inch (2.5 cm)

This loose assemblage of tiny corys does not always do well in a community tank as they often have trouble with bullying from larger species. When kept in a single-species tank with lots of java moss, they will readily reproduce, constantly adding to their frenetically busy school. At times and from a distance, they can be mistaken for characins as they are among the small group of midwater-swimming catfish. The pygmy corys are best kept in as large a school as possible.

Brochis splendens—the Common Brochis, the Emerald Brochis, Green Hump Catfish

(Castelnau 1855)
Peru, Ecuador
3 to 4 inches (8 to 10 cm)

If a *Corydoras* like *C. sterbai* can be said to be built like a bus, then the closely related brochis are double-deckers. These are extremely robust, heavy-bodied fish with an unexpected emerald sheen to their armored flanks. These gentle giants are not often kept because they are large schooling fish. At times, juveniles can be found misidentified as *Corydoras aeneus*. In a large aquarium, a school of any of the *Brochis* species is a wonderful sight.

Aspidoras

Aspidoras are an assemblage of cory-like catfish, with much of the interesting behavior of their cousins but little of the outward charm. While the large eyes and "winking" behavior of corys makes converts of many who stop to observe them in aquarium shops, *Aspidoras* are nicely patterned but somewhat pig-eyed rarities in the trade. They have attractive patterning. In a tank with a current and

good oxygen levels, they exhibit a level of activity that makes even the busiest cory look sleepy. The many species of these dynamic catfish are hard to tell apart unless you can get information on their origins. Whatever their Latin name, they can be kept and bred like corys if you respect their need for water flow. No aquarist who enjoys cory keeping should ever pass up a chance to keep these fish.

Porthole Catfish

The final group of armored cats we will look at are the rarely imported porthole catfish.

Dianema urostriata—the Flagtail Porthole Catfish

(Ribeiro 1912)
Rio Negro, Brazil
To 5 inches (13 cm)

This striking catfish is best kept in small troops of 6 to 12 animals. They are shy but can be kept in a community with some larger but nonaggressive tetras and cichlids. In nature they inhabit blackwater habitats with lots of wood and leaf litter where they look for food items such as worms and insect larvae. In practical terms, this survival strategy means *Dianema* are not well suited for planted tanks because their digging habits may uproot plants. Tanks with porthole cats are often cloudy as they constantly dig up the bottom in search of food.

Additional Resources

Nothing ever stands still in the world of catfish. As long as an aquarist decides to keep these curious fish, the temptation to learn about them will constantly reappear. Information will be modified, ranges of fish will be extended, and new things will be learned.

The Internet seems to have come along at the right time for catfish keepers, as its early days corresponded to the early days of the catfish explosion. For searches, you should work from the Latin names of the species that interest you to avoid the plethora of poor quality sites that are out there. To focus your exploration of catfish, you may want to consult the following resources:

Internet Sites

http://www.scotcat.com

http://www.planetcatfish.com

http://lists.aquaria.net/fish/catfish/
The Catfish Mailing List

http://www.corydoras.pwp.blueyonder.co.uk/
Ian Fuller's *Corydoras* Resource

http://george.cosam.auburn.edu/usr/key_to_loricariidae/lorhome/lorhome.html
The *Loricariids* Homepage by Jon Armbruster, Auburn University

http://tiger.towson.edu/~hnonog1/
Hiro Nonogaki's Panaque Homepage

http://tolweb.org/tree/
Tree of Life Webpage, Full of Catfish Info

Books

Baensch, H. A., and R. Riehl. *Aquarium Atlas,* Volumes 1–3.

Evers, Hans Georg and Seidel, Ingo. *Wels Atlas Band 1,* Mergus Verlag, Melle, 2002.

Fuller, I. A. M. *Breeding Corydoradine Catfishes,* Ian Fuller Enterprises, Kidderminster, U.K., 2001.

Glaser, Ulrich. *AQUALOG All Corydoras.*

Glaser, Ulrich. *AQUALOG Loricariidae: All L-numbers.*

Kobayagawa, M. *The World of Catfishes,* TFH, NJ, 1991.

Scheurmann, I. *Aquarium Fish Breeding,* Barron's Educational Series, Inc., Hauppauge, NY, 1990.

Smith, M. *Lake Tanganyika Cichlids,* Barron's Educational Series, Inc., Hauppauge, NY, 1998.

Zurlo, G. *The Tanganyika Cichlid Aquarium,* Barron's Educational Series, Inc., Hauppauge, NY, 2000.

Corydoras pantanalensis.

An Amazon sunset brings out many nocturnal cats.

Important Note

Electrical equipment for aquarium care is described in this book. Please do not fail to read the note below, since otherwise serious accidents could occur.

Water damage from broken glass, over-flowing, or tank leaks cannot always be avoided. Therefore, you should not fail to take out insurance.

Please take special care that neither children not adults ever eat any aquarium plants. It can result in serious health consequences. Fish medications should always be kept away from children.

Safety Around the Aquarium

Water and electricity can lead to dangerous accidents. Therefore you should make absolutely sure when buying equipment that it is suitable for use in an aquarium.

✔ Every technical device must have the UL sticker on it. These letters give the assurance that the safety of the equipment has been carefully checked by experts and that "with ordinary use" (as the experts say) nothing dangerous can happen.

✔ Always unplug any electrical equipment before you do any cleaning around or in the aquarium.

✔ Never do your own repairs on the aquarium or the equipment if there is something wrong with it. As a matter of safety, all repairs should only be carried out by an expert.

Acknowledgments

We would like to thank the following people, in no particular order, for helping with the book through their generous sharing of information, through their support, or through their helping us obtain some of the catfish shown in this book: Hiro Nonogaki, Francois Archambault, Brian Menard, Thomas Stoll, Ingo Seidel, Hans Georg Evers, Pete Liptrot, Shane Linder, Julius Dignall, Andy Taylor, Tsz Yin Lew, Ian Fuller, Keisuke Onoda, Dirk Ottlik, Laurence Azoulay, Mary Frauley, Roland Numrich, Ricardo Fridegotto, Segundo Laulate, Lee Finley, Eric Bodrock, Fred Schneider, Phil Oakes, Claude Gagnon, Hans Behr, and Mike Downey.

About the Authors

Oliver Lucanus is a writer, filmmaker, and wildlife photographer. He has traveled extensively throughout the tropics, both on scientific expeditions and fish-collecting trips for Belowwater, his tropical fish importing business.

Gary Elson is a teacher and a writer of both fiction and aquarium-related articles and books.

Photo Credits

All photos by Oliver Lucanus.

Cover Photos

All photos by Oliver Lucanus.

All inquiries should be addressed to:
Barron's Educational Series, Inc.
250 Wireless Boulevard
Hauppauge, NY 11788
http://www.barronseduc.com

International Standard Book No. 0-7641-2397-1

Library of Congress Catalog Card No. 2002043787

Library of Congress Cataloging-in-Publication Data
Elson, Gary.
　Catfish : everything about natural history, purchase, health, care, breeding, and species identification / Gary Elson and Oliver Lucanus.
　　p. cm. — (A complete pet owner's manual)
　Includes bibliographical references (p.).
　ISBN 0-7641-2397-1
　　1. Catfishes—Juvenile literature. 2. Aquariums—Juvenile literature. I. Lucanus, Oliver. II. Title. III. Series.

SF458.C38E48　2003
639.3'7492—dc21　　　　　　2002043787

Printed in Hong Kong
9 8 7 6 5 4 3 2 1